Chicago Tribune

Believe It!

The Story of Chicago's World Champions

Pitcher Mark Buehrle lets loose with the champagne at Minute Maid Park in Houston after the White Sox won the World Series.

Chicago Tribune

This book is available in quantity at special discounts for your group or organization. For further information, contact:

Triumph Books
542 S. Dearborn St.
Suite 750
Chicago, IL 60605
Phone: (312) 939-3330
Fax: (312) 663-3557

Printed in the United States of America

Joe Crede tags out Darin Erstad of the Angels, who was trying to stretch a double into a triple during Game 3 of the ALCS. The postseason allowed a national audience to see what made the White Sox a winner: defense, pitching and timely hitting.

Contents

Cubs town? Think again

I was walking to my car parked on 35th Street, about a mile west of the ballpark, in the midst of thousands of joyous fans. It was after the first World Series game, a 5-3 victory over Houston, and the fans, as they marched under the long railroad bridge, were shouting, "Go! White Sox! Go!" Followed by the chant, "Three more! Three more!"

And it occurred to me that the sportswriters and other miscellaneous soothsayers were all wrong, myself included, when they repeatedly insisted Chicago was a Cubs town. Never again. Even if the Cubs continue to outdraw the White Sox.

Chicago is a two-team city, always has been and always will be, one team up, the other down. The attendance figures are not an accurate index of the faithful and the passion. I hope the White Sox no longer will be described as the second team. And everyone under the 35th Street bridge would agree.

Some Cubs fans, we were told, were unable to root for the White Sox. I feel sorry for them. They missed out on the fun, and more important, an unforgettable Chicago experience.

And then driving home I saw the big Loop office buildings lit up with messages cheering the White Sox. If the Cubs win the pennant, and they will, I can't envision a bigger display. It was a wonderful time not only for the South Side but for the entire Chicago area.

This souvenir book is a review of the magical season. But it wasn't a miracle. The Sox had the best team.

I was in my third year as a baseball writer when they won the pennant in 1959, and I remember thinking, "This is great. Only three years on the beat and I've got a team in the World Series."

They didn't make it again for 46 years. It was worth the wait.

Jerome Holtzman

Former Chicago Tribune columnist Jerome Holtzman, an award-winning baseball writer, is a member of the Baseball Hall of Fame.

Paper may yellow, but magical season will be clear forever

By John Kass

That Tribune sports section from Oct. 27 that I'll be saving—perhaps in an envelope stuffed into a drawer with other White Sox World Series artifacts—will eventually turn yellow and old.

Maybe you're the kind of person who won't save any information that doesn't fit on a computer disk. I understand. You probably don't want to be some kind of pack rat.

But many of us will save the paper, the real paper, the real thing that you can hold in your hands, and this book on the Sox, too, and other stuff from this magical season.

Like tickets from games you've attended at Sox Park this year, with the names of people who sat with you written on the stubs, and box scores of those games taped to the tickets.

In that drawer, in the envelope underneath the good silver, the paper will become forgotten, brittle and crumbly at the edges, like pressed wedding flowers, delicate and strange to the touch.

There's nothing wrong with brittle. It's merely a symptom of time. Your hands will be brittle, too, if you're lucky enough to get old.

And some afternoon, while you're rooting about for something you've lost, you'll open the drawer and spot the envelope, surprised at first but knowing immediately what's in there.

You'll notice those older hands of yours extending into the drawer, as they reach back to a time when your hands were different and flexible, to that last week in October 2005, when the White Sox finally won the World Series.

This is baseball as time machine. You reach back and it brings you there.

Aside from the artifacts and clippings and the stuff, what memories have you put in there of this incredible season?

Naturally, the image of the Sox running out onto the infield at Minute Maid Park in Houston, the celebration with the guys jumping up, arms extended, the fans dancing, those late-night phone calls to your family and friends, an 88-year dry spell ended.

I figure you also stole a quiet moment away from the noise, to be still for a bit, to think about the great Sox fans you've known who didn't live to see this.

Time to consider all those who are South Siders in geography or spirit or both, pegged as second-class fans for years, all our social grievances weighing us down, imaginary gripes and real ones. And that chip was always on our shoulder, as we watched the Sox play ball in 2005 the way the South Side fans were taught to idealize the game: Fundamentals, pitching and incredible defense, and power too.

This White Sox team not only won the Series, which would have been enough for us, but in doing so became one of the great teams.

It was a season of tightness, always edgy, brilliantly played but never relaxing. We fans buzzed through a near-crash in Septem-

Beverly neighbors watch their team in the fourth game of the World Series on a projection screen set up in a yard.

ber as manager Ozzie Guillen held the team and us together, and then the playoffs and World Series, as we subsisted on the official Sox fan vitamins: caffeine, adrenaline and anxiety.

"Did we ever have a laugher, a relaxing game, not counting the playoff game against Boston with all the home runs?" asked my cousin George, who shares season-ticket seats with me along the first-base line. "I mean, every game was close, every game was a squeaker. We can't take it anymore."

We don't have to—not until pitchers and catchers report to spring training next year.

We devoured every bit of information in the papers, on TV, venting at the critics who figured their job was to gin up anger among us with declarations that this team would choke. It didn't choke.

And while the memories should be about the players, and the games and our families and friends who shared it, I've got two other memories to press in there too.

One was Sox Chairman Jerry Reinsdorf crying as he was awarded the championship trophy. He's brought more cham-

pionship trophies to Chicago than any other owner, although now he has brought the one that counts. It's time Chicago appreciates Reinsdorf for what he's done.

And general manager Ken Williams, a former Sox player who once tried to make the ballclub on a broken ankle, lacing a puffy foot into his spikes and refusing to quit. As GM, he had the guts to change a team of thumpers into a team that played baseball, and risked his job and his reputation by dumping popular sluggers who played for themselves so he could generate the cash needed to sign pitchers like El Duque.

Williams was in the dugout at Sox Park back in May when I asked him whether he'd ever get some respect in Chicago.

"Respect?" he said then. "This is Chicago. To get respect in this city, to create that groundswell with fans, you've got to win it all. We know it. We don't have a problem with that. That's the way it is. You win, you get respect."

It's about time. ◆

Best way to enjoy incredible journey: Suspend disbelief

By Rick Morrissey

It figures. I can't get that stupid Journey song out of my mind. I'm writing this in the afterglow of the White Sox's 1-0 victory over Houston to win the World Series for the first time in 88 years. It's late, and no one should have to live with these lyrics rattling inside his or her cage:

Just a small-town girl, livin' in a lonely world
She took the midnight train goin' anywhere
Just a city boy, born and raised in south Detroit
He took the midnight train goin' anywhere

Ah, the things we'll sing to lure a World Series championship to this town. And so "Don't Stop Believin'," the Sox's unofficial postseason theme song, is stalking me like an ax murderer because A.J. Pierzynski, Aaron Rowand and Joe Crede had a few too many drinks one night and asked the lounge singer to play anything by Journey.

Well, you know what they say, Chicago: No pain, no gain.

The truth is, this whole thing still feels so unreal, I can't stop disbelievin'. A city that was a baseball ghost town now has a world championship, via a sweep of the Astros. It seems unthinkable, but think again: It's here, and it's real.

The last time the Sox won a World Series was 1917. We have been conditioned ever since to believe that it would never happen again. We were Loserville. The Cubs were a lost cause, and the Sox didn't have the imagination or the money or the owner to do things right. That was the thinking.

But along came a manager who brought belief and a wagging tongue to the equation. Ozzie Guillen was so crazy, so smart, so silly and so wily that you couldn't help but follow him. You wanted to see what he would say or do next.

Along came a general manager who not only wasn't afraid to make a deal but seemed to live for the wheeling and the dealing. The one deal Ken Williams couldn't make—to get Ken Griffey Jr. from Cincinnati—might have been the best thing that happened to this team. This was a club built on a delicate chemistry. Whatever the mixture was, it worked. Williams gets the credit for that.

He put together a pitching staff that other teams dreamed of and feared, and the proof was in the American League Championship Series, when Mark Buehrle, Jon Garland, Freddy Garcia and Jose Contreras threw consecutive complete-game victories. Crazy. Absolutely crazy.

Williams is the one who took a chance on a pudgy reliever named Bobby Jenks, who was brought up to the bigs in July and was their closer in the playoffs.

Williams is the one who took a chance on Pierzynski, the catcher with a reputation for being a cancer in the clubhouse after a bad stint with the Giants. What Pierzynski turned out to be was a free radical, running around like a madman and leading the Sox in heart and controversy.

World Series Most Valuable Player Jermaine Dye, who hit .438 over the four games, is congratulated by teammates.

The momentum-turner in the playoffs was the dropped-third-strike incident in Game 2 of the ALCS, when Angels catcher and former Sox Josh Paul rolled the ball back to the mound on what he thought was a strikeout to end the ninth inning. But umpire Doug Eddings ruled, probably erroneously, that the ball had hit the dirt first and that Pierzynski, who had alertly sprinted to first, was safe.

And the Sox had enough life left to win that game.

No doubt, fate was on the Sox's side. Fate—that thing that always spikes Chicago baseball teams in the shins—finally sided with the club from the South Side. Crazy. Absolutely crazy.

But the thought that this might have been preordained lessens the accomplishment, doesn't it? This was a team that had to battle a lot of things this season but mostly itself in the dog days of summer. You don't go from 15 games up in your division to 1½ games up in late September to a World Series title and then attribute it all to fate. That's not fair. That takes away from the prize.

Before we think about the big-ticket items—Scott Podsednik's game-winning homer in Game 2 or Geoff Blum's 14th-inning homer in Game 3—let's not forget Juan Uribe's steadiness at shortstop in the postseason or Tadahito Iguchi's wonderful regular season. How about what Neal Cotts did in relief in Game 2 to set up Jenks' 100-m.p.h. heroics to beat the Astros? Not bad.

Paul Konerko became a star in these playoffs, and Joe Crede became a man, shaking off a below-average regular season at the plate to pound four homers in the postseason. Oh, and he was Brooks Robinson at third too.

Blum, who had one at-bat in the playoffs until his game-win-

ning homer, was Williams' only acquisition before the trading deadline. Guess that deal worked out pretty well, huh?

There were so many players who had a role in this thing. Jermaine Dye, the World Series Most Valuable Player with a .438 average. Willie Harris, with the single and the winning run in Game 4. Rowand. Dustin Hermanson. Cliff Politte. Frank Thomas, the face of this organization for so long, was a home-run machine for a brief while before fate said his ankle wasn't going to hold up. His ring means just as much as anybody else's. Come to think of it, so does Chairman Jerry Reisndorf's.

At one point late in the regular season, Guillen said he would quit if the Sox won the World Series. That seems very, very unlikely now for the simple reason that Guillen would have to hire people with notebooks and cameras to record his every word. He loves talking. Don't go, Ozzie. This way is so much cheaper.

People have very distinct memories of this World Series and especially Game 3, the 5-hour-41-minute mini-series. But for me it's a blur, and what I remember, I remember in snippets. As Blum came to bat in the 14th inning, I remember turning to my colleague, Mike Downey, and saying, "Does Geoff Blum have any power?" I remember Blum hitting that homer to right and Downey replying, "So, you were saying?"

Because of deadline constraints, I had to file three columns that night: a Sox lose column, which never ran; a Sox victory column that made about 75 percent of the papers delivered the next day; and a Dewey-ties-Truman column that ran in about 25 percent of the papers. I remember wishing I could have captured something of what I had just seen.

Because I'm still not believin' what I think I saw. ◆

Follow time line to make sense of timeless season

By Mike Downey

April 4, St. Louis

Hate to miss the first White Sox home game. I wonder if they'll be worth a darn this year.

I need to be here in St. Louis because tonight, the Illinois Fighting Illini are going to play North Carolina for college basketball's national championship. It sure would be cool to see a team from my home state win a championship in something, wouldn't it?

April 5, St. Louis

Well, a shame about the Illini. I like what I hear from yesterday's Sox game, however. A 1-0 win over Cleveland? (I guess the Indians won't be heard from much this season.) Whole game's over in 1 hour 51 minutes. Man, that Mark Buehrle ... he works faster than Tough-Actin' Tinactin.

Oh, and a save for Shingo Takatsu too. I bet he saves 30 games, maybe 40.

April 7, Chicago

Three homers off Shingo by the Indians in the ninth inning? Ow. Well, you can't win 'em all.

April 25, Oakland

Well, you can win almost all. After 20 games, the Sox are 16-4. Is this a tease? They even beat Oakland today in Oakland. (May I burn my copy of "Moneyball" now?)

April 27, Oakland

Oops, I remember now why the Sox hate this place. Aaron Rowand loses a fly ball in the sun. Joe Crede is hit by a pitch, but the plate umpire overturns it. (Why won't an ump ever give a Sox guy a break?) Ozzie Guillen, ejected. Crede, ejected. Chris Widger, a catcher, has to play third base. Jermaine Dye, a right fielder, goes to shortstop for the first time in his pro career.

This could be a weird year.

May 6, Kansas City

Paul Konerko is 0 for 23. His average is .190. Won't this guy ever get another hit?

May 14, Chicago

The Sox have held leads in 37 games in a row. This is wild. Scott Podsednik steals four bases in one day. (And if he wears his socks any higher, they'll be leotards.)

May 22, North Side of Chicago

Brandon McCarthy vs. Mark Prior? A question: Brandon who? He's how old—21? I wear socks that old. But, hey, the kid looks all right. Gives up four hits at Wrigley, pitches into the sixth. Looks pretty good after the game too. Sox teammates haze him, make him wear a dress. (This episode of "Sox Sex and the City" is rated PG-13.)

June 8, Denver

Here are the happy totals: 15 runs, 22 hits, back-to-back homers in the ninth by Crede and the Big Hurt. (He's back!) Cliff Politte even got a hit. Sox's record is 40-19 now. Wow.

Pitchers Jon Garland and Dustin Hermanson douse each other with bubbly in the locker room after the 1-0 victory by the White Sox to capture the World Series over the Houston Astros.

June 18, Chicago

Look who's here-the Dodgers, daring to set foot on the South Side for the first time since 1959. And it looks bad for the Sox today ... until A.J. Pierzynski's walk-off homer caps a four-run ninth. Take that, L.A. This year we're the ones going to the World Series. (Ha, ha, ha.)

July 12, Detroit

Buehrle starts the All-Star Game for the American League (and wins it). You know what this means? If the White Sox go to the World Series, they have home-field advantage. (Ha, ha, ha.)

July 18, Chicago

Sox win fifth in a row. They now are 62-29. This is ridiculous. Big Hurt hits his 12th homer. (Yes, he's definitely back.)

July 21, Chicago

Big Hurt is hurt. Heads to DL. Will not be back. There goes the Sox's season, probably.

July 31, Baltimore

At the trade deadline, we get ... Ken Griffey Jr.? Uh, no. Jeff Blum. Or is it Geoff Blum? Oh, it doesn't matter. That's the last you'll hear of him.

Aug. 1, Baltimore

They let Takatsu go? No way. His slow stuff made batters freeze. (All this boy Bobby Jenks has is a fastball.)

Aug. 30, Arlington, Texas

McCarthy hurls 7 2/3 scoreless innings for his first big-league win. When the Sox go to the playoffs, this kid's going with them.

Sept. 7, Chicago

Sox now 36 games over .500. And yesterday's attendance? A sellout? SRO? Uh, no: 14,571.

Sept. 18, Minneapolis

Ross Gload scores game-winner and Twins fall 2-1, but it's Cleveland breathing down our necks. And the Tribe comes to the Cell tomorrow. No way the Sox can blow this . . . can they?

Sept. 29, Detroit

I haven't seen this much champagne since I went to Liza Minnelli's last wedding. Sox clinch the playoffs. Their fans chant: "Jerry! Jerry! Jerry!" I wonder if they mean Springer.

Oct. 2, Cleveland

Sox get victory No. 99. It's a happy ballclub, except for some of the subs who overheard a radio guy calling them "scrubs." (I doubt if guys like Blum will be needed in the playoffs, though.)

Oct. 7, Boston

Out go the old Sox, in go the new. Na, na, hey, hey, kiss those 2004 champs goodbye.

Oct. 16, Anaheim

Rain. Lightning. Thunder. I hate California ... it's cold and it's damp. Meanwhile, the Sox win the pennant! (Don't these guys ever do anything big at home?)

Oct. 23, Chicago

Konerko—not just a homer, not just a grand slam, but a World Series grand slam. Podsednik—not just a homer, not just a walk-off homer, but a World Series walk-off homer. Holy #%!*#!

Oct. 25, Houston

A 5-hour-41-minute game? The longest in a World Series ever? Won on a home run by Blum ... in his first Series at-bat? I wave the white sock of surrender. I've seen it all now.

Oct. 26, Houston

The perfect ending. White Sox win 1-0 ... the same score as Opening Day. ◆

The sight of Scott Podsednik stealing a base became a recurring theme of the 2005 season, and his speed served as a table-setter for the White Sox's new-look offense.

Mark Buehrle encourages Joe Crede to take a curtain call after a three-run homer put the Sox on top of Detroit during a July contest.

Water drips from the head of Jose Contreras as he cools himself in the dugout during a Sox loss to the Angels on June 1.

The spring training promise of a reconfigured team included the bat, glove and experience of veteran Jermaine Dye.

Freddy Garcia, acquired in a midseason 2004 trade, provided part of the pitching foundation on which a championship team was built.

Catcher Chris Widger congratulates Mark Buehrle for tossing a 1-hour-39-minute gem against Seattle in April.

Manager Ozzie Guillen with team Chairman Jerry Reinsdorf at spring training in Tucson, Ariz.

Beautiful grind

Playing 'small ball' pays big dividends on march to title

By Dan McGrath

Ozzie Guillen is known for speaking his mind, and he was adamant and specific when his boss, Ken Williams, asked what type of team he'd like to put on the field for his second season as White Sox manager.

"Get me pitching, speed and defense," Guillen said.

Williams, in his fifth season as Sox general manager, didn't have to be persuaded. Weary of seeing a plodding, cumbersome team slug its way to only modest results, he was of a mind to assemble a lineup capable of manufacturing runs. One that could make things happen and put pressure on opponents rather than sit back and wait for the long ball. One that could catch the ball and make life easier for a promising group of pitchers.

And he wanted something more. He wanted passion.

"I wanted guys who were more concerned with wins and losses than individual numbers, guys who took it personally when we lost and weren't happy about it," Williams said. "People would come up to me all the time and tell me, 'I've been a White Sox fan all my life, and I'd sure like to see them in a World Series.'

"I heard it so often that it struck a chord with me. More than ever, I saw it as my mission to give those people a team they could be proud of."

Thus the advent of "grinder ball." It was more than a marketing slogan; it was a style of play. The question was: Did the Sox have the personnel to make that style work? Williams and Guillen didn't think so.

So Williams, never shy about making a move, endeavored to reconstruct the roster. Considering they'd won 83 games in 2004 and had gone five years without a losing record, the Sox underwent a fairly substantial off-season makeover.

Magglio Ordoñez, a popular and productive right fielder, was allowed to depart as a free agent. He was coming off a serious knee injury, and the Sox not only had concerns about his long-term health, they had other plans for the money he was seeking.

Shortstop Jose Valentin, a shaky fielder on his best days, also left as a free agent.

The most significant move involved left fielder Carlos Lee.

SEE PAGE 28 ▶

Ken Williams

When people were tugging at them from all different directions and calling them chokers and everything else, they never lost their togetherness. That impressed me more than their record.

We're conditioned in this town to expect the worst. Because that's what's happened. Call it as you see it. So in order to change that, you have to have fighters who have a little edge about them, that have been doubted all their lives, all their careers because they have overcome that stuff before

and they have an attitude that they can again.

When that man[1] sat down in front of me and he didn't have a job and he wanted that job desperately, I told him: "Hey, you've got a lot of convincing to do. I love you like a brother, but you have a lot of convincing to do if I'm going to put my reputation on the line and give you this job." And basically we started a 20-minute argument. He told me: "You know me. If you don't think I can do the job, let me know right now and I'll get up and go back to Miami. Don't waste my time." I told him

Oct. 9 in the dugout at U.S. Cellular Field.

"What'd you come for if you're going to quit that easy?"

If he's not afraid to fight me when he doesn't have the job, then we're going to make some good decisions together. He ain't going to tell me what I want to hear.

I feel a sense of responsibility to him[2], and I feel a sense of responsibility to these fans who've been waiting for 30, 40, 50 years.

I don't have all the answers. Anybody who tells you they have the answers in this game, you better run as fast as you can in the opposite direction.

[1] *Ozzie Guillen.* [2] *Jerry Reinsdorf.*

27

FROM PAGE 25

Williams realized that .300 hitters with 30-homer power didn't just fall out of trees, but Lee's shortcomings in the field and on the bases made him a poor fit for the type of team Williams and Guillen envisioned.

Milwaukee, which valued Lee's big bat, offered outfielder Scott Podsednik and pitcher Luis Vizcaino, and Williams was willing to sacrifice Lee's power for an opportunity to add a speedy leadoff hitter and a durable bullpen arm.

There were financial considerations as well. Unloading the contracts of Ordóñez, Lee and Valentin gave Williams the flexibility to address other needs.

Right fielder Jermaine Dye, signed as a free agent, offered power comparable to Ordóñez's at a fraction of the cost. Emboldened by the 2004 success of reliever Shingo Takatsu, Williams looked to Japan again and came up with second baseman Tadahito Iguchi, which enabled him to move Juan Uribe to shortstop to replace Valentin and upgrade the defense.

Dustin Hermanson was an inexpensive addition to the bullpen, and Orlando "El Duque" Hernandez was not only a veteran presence on the pitching staff but a source of comfort and support for Cuban countryman Jose Contreras.

Finally, Williams let bygones be bygones and offered the catching job to A.J. Pierzynski. A world-class irritant in his days with Minnesota, Pierzynski seemed to be in the middle of everything that happened between the Twins and the White Sox as their rivalry escalated over the last few years. Many Sox players couldn't stand him.

But he was available at a bargain price after one unhappy season in San Francisco, and Williams believed Pierzynski's sturdy left-handed bat and ability to run a pitching staff outweighed his personality quirks. But even those quirks could prove useful.

SEE PAGE 32 ▶

Tadahito Iguchi was one of many new faces of 2005, and the second baseman showed
at the plate and in the field why he had been a four-time Japanese Pacific League all-star.

Ozzie Guillen

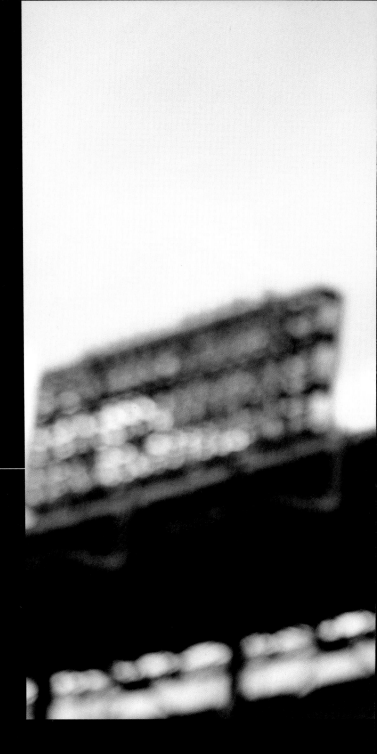

Last year I wasn't managing. I was just changing pitchers. That's it. I feel like a manager this year. I feel like I have a better chance to do a lot of different things. I have the ammunition to do it and the players to do it.

Have a good pitching coach. The reason I like this team is that it doesn't have selfish players. We don't have anyone with an ego. The greatest man I ever met in my life[1]. Not because he's my boss. Because Jerry Reinsdorf is a straight man who will not lie to you. A lot of people should

know Jerry the way I know him. Jerry means well for everybody, especially this city. Jerry is treated so badly in this city. I think Jerry should be more loved, more respected.

Great[2]. Loyal. Patient. Lot of patience. I believe a lot of kids look up to us. They say, "You are my hero." I say, "Thank you, but your mother and father should be your heroes."

Winning the World Series[3] was part of my

Oct. 9 at U.S. Cellular Field.

dreams. There's no better feeling in baseball. When they hired me, they didn't hire me to build a team, they hired me to win. And if we don't win, it's Ozzie Guillen's fault.

The players win games, managers lose games. That's the way I think, because when you're losing, who gets fired? If we don't play good, I'll be the first one to tell Jerry and Kenny[4] to get another one. I'm the first White Sox fan, besides being the manager. I want the White Sox to win with me or without me.

I wish we could win with me.

1 *Jerry Reinsdorf.* 2 *Sox fans.* 3 *When he coached third base for the Florida Marlins in 2003.* 4 *Ken Williams.*

Jon Garland blazed out of the gate as the No. 5 starter, going 8-0 before taking his first loss May 23.

FROM PAGE 28

Like him or not, Pierzynski was all about winning, and Williams believed his team needed a little more edge.

"I like our club," Guillen said as Opening Day approached.

What was not to like? Steady Mark Buehrle and Takatsu combined on a two-hitter in a snappy 1 hour 51 minutes to beat Cleveland 1-0 on Opening Day, a performance that set the tone for the rest of the season. The Sox took the lead in the American League Central, and they would not relinquish it over the next six months, going wire to wire to win their first division title since 2000.

The first of three eight-game winning streaks highlighted a 17-7 April. The Sox began to establish dominance in the division by going 14-4 against AL Central teams, and while their lone West Coast trip was typically tough, a 2-1 loss April 27 at Oakland had an upside. Injuries and ejections caused some lineup manipulation, and the game ended with Dye at shortstop and backup catcher Chris Widger at third base, suggesting the roster was both deep and flexible.

Carl Everett was the Sox's most productive April hitter, with 20 RBIs in 23 games. Iguchi showed he wouldn't be overmatched against major-league pitching, batting .333 with 26 hits, and Paul Konerko slugged seven April homers.

Jon Garland began the season as the No. 5 starter, but he immediately began demonstrating the capabilities of an ace in his sixth major-league season, winning his four April starts with a 1.80 earned-run average and one shutout.

SEE PAGE 37 ▶

A roster gamble that paid off for the '05 Sox, catcher A.J. Pierzynski revels in a 10th-inning walk-off homer by Joe Crede on Sept. 20 against Cleveland.

Mark Buehrle

I never really believed in chemistry until this year. Just with the guys who are in the clubhouse. It may be because we're winning games, but off the field, when we have a day game and an off day, there's so many guys who go out and eat dinner together.

When they kept on getting rid of all our offensive power and saying we're going pitching and defense, the first thing is, you realize you don't want that to happen. You want 10 runs a game. But it's worked out for us.

In spring training, everybody thinks their team has on paper what it takes to get to the postseason. But I don't think anybody expected us—and I don't think anybody in this clubhouse expected us—to start out this hot.

A lot of different things can happen when you get to the postseason. The wild-card teams have won it the last three years. So it doesn't matter if we go out there and win our division by 50 games and win 120 games, we just need to go out there and play in the postseason like we have all season long.

Feb. 26 at spring training in Tucson, Ariz.

I was raised in St. Charles, Mo. I've said it and I'm going to stick by it until the day I die: I've always wanted to play for the Cardinals, but the White Sox gave me a chance to play professional baseball. I'm going to honor my contract, and if they come to me and want to sign me again and it works out for both of us, then I'm going to sign here. I'd love to finish my career as a White Sox.

Don't take it for granted. Enjoy it while you're here. There's tons of people who want to be out there in my shoes.

Grill your own tailgate banquet outside the ballpark and wash it down with a victory—like the 47 home wins served up by the Sox to go along with 34 losses. The team's road record was even more impressive at 52-29.

Scott Podsednik slides in ahead of the tag of Baltimore catcher Javy Lopez. The speedy left fielder, acquired from the Brewers, sparked the offense by scoring 80 runs, second only to slugger Paul Konerko's 98.

FROM PAGE 32

May was the month in which the Sox learned they had something special in Podsednik. In tandem with Iguchi, he gave them the "get 'em on, get 'em over, get 'em in" presence at the top of the order they had sought.

Podsednik had 31 hits and 12 walks in 28 games in the month for a .383 on-base percentage. He stole 16 bases, scored 17 runs and became a crowd favorite with his hustle and verve as the Sox went 18-10 in May and stretched their division lead to five games over the Twins.

But it wasn't all "small ball." Dye and Pierzynski hit seven home runs apiece and Konerko added six as the Sox pounded out 36 homers in 28 May games. They won two of three from the Cubs at Wrigley Field in their first interleague venture, with Brandon McCarthy making his big-league debut.

And they ran their AL Central record to 18-4 as Garland stretched his winning streak to eight before losing and Buehrle went 4-0 in six starts. When Takatsu struggled in the closer's role, Hermanson got a chance and was 8 for 8 in save opportunities.

Perhaps the best news came on the final day of the month:

SEE PAGE 43 ▶

A.J. Pierzynski tags out Detroit's Carlos Guillen in a 7-5 victory in July. The White Sox feasted on Detroit and other Central Division opponents, going 52-22 and never losing possession of first place.

Aaron Rowand is saluted in the dugout after blasting a solo homer off the Yankees' Randy Johnson as the Sox knocked four out of the park in a single inning and ended an excruciating seven-game losing streak.

Frank Thomas' comeback from injury in June was power-intense. The Big Hurt knocked out 12 homers and drove in 26 runs in just 34 games.

Freddy Garcia

This season has been pretty fun. I try to do the job the best I can. I try to keep the guys in the game and throw a lot of innings.

I want to throw the ball. But baseball has changed a lot. We've got a good bullpen, so if you can go seven innings, you can go right to the bullpen. I've learned to pitch better. Before I used to throw really hard. Now I don't throw as hard, but I locate my fastball and breaking pitch better.

I was here the second half of the season[1], and now we have a bunch of new people. Last year maybe everybody was on different wavelengths.

This year everybody is more together. Sometimes when that happens, you get a good team. Guys stick together.

Ozzie is a really good friend. But we're playing ball. He does his job, I do mine. It's all about respect.

Oct. 7 at Fenway Park, Boston, after the ALDS sweep.

They called me and said, "Hey, you got traded."[2] "For who?" "You and Guillen and Halama[3] for Randy Johnson." I was like, that's cool. It was a really big deal. People wanted to talk to you about the trade.

I say my best baseball memory was in 2000 in Yankee Stadium, the playoffs, third game. I pitched really good.

[1] *In 2004 after being traded from Seattle to the White Sox.*
[2] *From Houston to Seattle.* [3] *Shortstop Carlos Guillen and pitcher John Halama.*

Dustin Hermanson celebrates after striking out the side in a 5-4 win over Toronto in August. Hermanson's 34 saves led the staff.

The Yankees' Robinson Cano beats the throw to Joe Crede in an August game. The White Sox and New York split their season series and didn't meet again in the postseason-to the dismay of some South Side faithful.

FROM PAGE 37

Frank Thomas, coming off surgery on a fractured foot, completed a minor-league rehabilitation assignment and was activated from the disabled list.

The Sox established that they were for real in June with an 18-7 record that featured another eight-game winning streak as well as a four-gamer. They led the division by as many as 10½ games and owned a nine-game advantage when the month ended.

The pitching remained stellar, never better than on June 6-7 in Denver. Freddy Garcia, Jose Contreras and the bullpen limited the Colorado Rockies to seven hits over back-to-back games, the lowest two-game total in the history of Coors Field, a hitter's paradise. Buehrle was named AL pitcher of the month for June after going 3-0 with an 0.96 ERA in five starts.

The Sox were 10-5 in interleague games, including a three-game sweep of the Dodgers highlighted by the first walk-off home run of Pierzynski's career, a two-run shot that capped a

four-run ninth inning for a 5-3 win June 18. People were starting to notice. The crowd of 36,067 that night was one of six in excess of 30,000 they drew in the month.

Frank Thomas? He was around—eight home runs, 13 RBIs and a .698 slugging percentage in 19 June games.

July brought the All-Star break, and while the Sox limped into it by losing a three-game series to Oakland, they still had a 57-29 record, the best first-half showing in franchise history. And they charged out of the break, sweeping a four-game set at Cleveland.

The break itself was a time to savor that remarkable first half. Their record was the best in baseball, and they led the division by nine games.

Konerko, Garland and Buehrle were chosen for the All-Star Game; Buehrle became the starting and winning pitcher. Meanwhile, Sox fans showed their appreciation for Podsednik by selecting him for the final at-large roster spot with nearly

SEE PAGE 48 ▶

43

Mark Buehrle gives the fans something extra to cheer about on a blistering June afternoon. The Sox gave the home crowd even more to celebrate by trouncing the crosstown rival Cubs 12-2.

Paul Konerko reaches for the plate around Boston's Doug Mirabelli in a July game. Konerko lost the battle, but the Sox won 8-4 and showed for the first time they could hold their own against the 2004 World Series champions.

Aaron Rowand

I think I enjoy watching a good catch more than I enjoy watching myself hit a home run on TV. It's more exciting. It's more fun for me because I take pride in playing defense.

I think it's just chemistry with the guys here. We've got a great group of guys that enjoy being around each other.

I'd like to see us go all the way to the World Series.

You can understand most of what he[1] says. Sometimes you don't. Sometimes he'll come up and say something and walk away, and you'll turn to the guy next to you and go, "What'd he just say? I didn't get that one."

Everybody knows he's joking and he keeps things loose, but when it's time for him to put his foot down, there's no doubt you know who's in charge.

I feel like I've swung the bat a little bit better.

Oct. 20 at practice U.S. at Cellular Field.

I think I spent the first half of the season trying to find what I had last season and I threw it out the window. I didn't feel real comfortable out of the gate. I got off to a slow start and started searching for things. I was searching for a feeling I had last season instead of trying to hit myself into a good feeling. You can't try to duplicate things all the time.

If you can't adjust up here, you're going to have a short stay.

I dreamed this, but I never imagined any of this would get to come true. I'm a lucky guy to do what I'm doing.

[1] *Ozzie Guillen.*

The American League-leading White Sox boasted four All-Stars—Paul Konerko, Jon Garland, Mark Buehrle and Scott Podsednik—for the July game at Comerica Park in Detroit. It marked the Sox's largest All-Star delegation since 1975. Buehrle started for the AL and was credited with the win.

FROM PAGE 43

4 million votes after a "vote early and often" campaign that was typical Chicago. The four-man All-Star delegation was the Sox's largest since 1975.

The Sox hit the 100-game mark with a 65-35 record and an 11½-game lead. They showed they could play with the AL East heavyweights, splitting four games with defending World Series champion Boston on July 21-24. The series drew 150,871 fans, largest turnout for a four-gamer at U.S. Cellular Field since 1994.

Despite suffering spider bites that caused him to miss the Boston series, Dye hit five homers and drove in 22 runs in July. The only drawback: Thomas fractured a different bone in his foot and was declared out for the season July 29. Efforts to add another hitter for the stretch drive were unavailing; utility player Geoff Blum, obtained from San Diego, was the only acquisition at the trading deadline.

The All-Star Game victory assured the American League home-field advantage in the World Series. With a 68-35 record and a 14½-game lead going into August, the Sox were beginning to think that might come in handy.

August offered a suggestion that the Sox had been making it look too easy as they finally deviated from their trademark consistency. The season's first trip to Yankee Stadium produced two wins in three well-played games. Aaron Rowand made a name for himself on the New York stage with a series of spectacular fielding plays in center field. Contreras, the ex-Yankee, won the middle game with seven innings of scoreless, three-hit pitching, typical of a second half in which he was the Sox's most effective starter.

But a seven-game losing streak followed as the Sox hit their first real rough patch. Back-to-back losses in Boston preceded a three-game sweep at home by the Twins, who were making noise about getting back into the division race after slicing the Sox's lead below double digits.

The skid reached seven when they managed only one run in two games against the Yankees, but they abruptly came out of their hitting funk with four fourth-inning homers off Randy Johnson in a 6-2 win Aug. 21 at the Cell.

The next game may well have been the toughest loss of the season: Garcia pitched a one-hitter but lost to the Twins and Johan Santana 1-0 on Jacque Jones' eighth-inning homer. If the Sox were demoralized, they shook it off quickly, reeling off

SEE PAGE 52 ▶

Carl Everett looks to the heavens after pumping his second home run of the night against the Twins in April.

Tadahito Iguchi

I had my experience in Japan and wanted to try my luck over here. I don't feel any pressure[1]. My manager at Daiei was Sadaharu Oh[2]. It's 180 degrees from playing under Ozzie. He wasn't really a jokester. He didn't have the same kind of relationship with the players that Ozzie does.

Ozzie is very close to the players, so they're able to have very good communication. He keeps himself close to the players. He doesn't keep himself aloof.

We're successful because everyone's doing what they have to do. Shingo[3] was always a help to me from when I first got here. I'm upset that he's gone now. We had a good relationship. I'm sad, but that's the way the world turns.

The biggest adjustment is taking so long to come to work—the traffic, and Schaumburg is such a long way. That distance is not something I was used to.

Oct. 9 at practice at U.S. Cellular Field.

I'm not cracking open the books for English. Around the clubhouse, I'm working on my understanding and trying to communicate with other players.

The baseball world is the same in Japan as it is here. As far as normal conversation, I can pick up what people are saying. In Japan, we are schooled in English.

When we won the Japanese World Series twice, those were my best baseball moments.

Winning the World Series here would rank first. That would be No. 1.

[1] *To play well and continue the progression to America of Japanese players.* [2] *Japan's all-time home run leader.* [3] *Former Sox relief pitcher Shingo Takatsu.*

FROM PAGE 48

four straight wins to salvage a 12-16 record in their first losing month of the season.

They were 29 games over .500 at 80-51 and held a seven-game lead in the division. Of more concern was the groin injury that sent Podsednik to the disabled list for the final two weeks of August. The Sox weren't the same team without him, and Hermanson was missing in action as well, victim of a cranky back that limited his availability.

The league had caught up with Takatsu, who was designated for assignment in July. So the closer's role fell to Bobby Jenks, a husky, hard-throwing 24-year-old with a nasty curve and a nasty disposition who'd begun the season in Double A.

Podsednik was back in September, and the Sox announced their intention to close strong by opening the month with seven straight wins. One was a 5-3 decision over Boston, a makeup game from an earlier rainout in which rookie McCarthy outpitched Curt Schilling. The next day they beat Kansas City and surpassed 2 million in home attendance for the first time since 1993.

But they couldn't seal the deal, dropping six of their next seven, including a three-game sweep by the Angels at home and prompting a "we flat-out stink" assessment from Guillen

SEE PAGE 55 ▶

Hitting coach Greg Walker and manager Ozzie Guillen monitor the proceedings in a tense extra-inning affair against the Twins.

Paul Konerko reacts after popping out with two men aboard in the ninth in a Sept. 19 loss to Cleveland. The Sox's loss and Cleveland's 14th win in 15 games brought the Indians within an uncomfortably close 2½ games.

The luck of the Irish fails to rub off as Aaron Rowand and the Sox fall to the Angels on the night of the Halfway to St. Patrick's Day promotion at U.S. Cellular Field.

A leaping Aaron Rowand couldn't snare this one but took many a homer away from opponents, whether on patrol at U.S. Cellular Field or on the road.

His 18 victories leading a staff ranked among baseball's best, Jon Garland has a chat on the mound with catcher A.J. Pierzynski.

FROM PAGE 52

after a loss to the lowly Royals in Kansas City. While Minnesota had fallen back, Cleveland had been coming on as the hottest team in baseball, and 13 of the Sox's final 17 games would be against the Twins and Indians.

They had no luck with Santana and were shut out 5-0 in the middle game of a three-game set Sept. 17 at the Metrodome, but they won the first and third games to set up a pivotal three-game series with the Indians on Sept. 19-21 in Chicago.

Cleveland took the opener 7-5 on Aaron Boone's two-run ninth-inning single off Jenks. The next night they played what might have been the game of the regular season.

The Indians could have crept within a game and a half with a victory, and they had a chance to break a 5-5 tie in the ninth inning with runners on first and third and two outs when Coco Crisp sent a sharp grounder into the hole. It looked for all the world like an RBI single, but Uribe backhanded the ball and nailed the speedy Crisp

with a miraculously strong throw. The tie was preserved … until the bottom of the 10th, when Crede sent the crowd home with a walk-off homer.

The Indians did draw within 1½ games by winning the series finale, which turned out to be their last gasp. They were beaten in Kansas City when center fielder Grady Sizemore lost a fly ball in the sun, and the Sox regrouped, winning three of four from the Twins at the Cell. The Sox stumbled twice in Detroit, but Cleveland couldn't take advantage against Tampa Bay, and when Garcia beat the Tigers 4-2 on Sept. 29, the Sox clinched the division.

The season-ending three-game series in Cleveland still had meaning because the Indians were chasing the AL wild-card berth, but the Sox ended those hopes with a three-game sweep that stretched their winning streak to five and suggested they were playoff-ready.

They were Central Division champions … and they were just getting started. ◆

Teammates wait to mob Joe Crede after his 10th-inning blast against Cleveland. Team celebrations were a common sight in 2005, with the Sox winning an MLB-best 35 one-run games.

Late-season addition Bobby Jenks came up big for the Sox and in the hearts of fans. The 270-pound flamethrower saved six games in the stretch run.

Sox fans are always proud to wear the colors, even more so in 2005.

Joe Crede

I thought we were definitely going to have a good team because of our pitching coming out of spring training. It was just a matter of everybody staying healthy and pitching the way they knew how to pitch. That was the big thing.

Toward the end of the season, we kind of hit a bump in the road there, and Cleveland got within a game and a half. But we showed a lot of guts and heart at the end. We won five in a row. Showed a lot of guts and heart. We just went back to our fundamental way of playing baseball.

Hitting the home run against Cleveland this year. It was the bottom of the ninth. That was when they were coming back. They had gained all the ground on us. It was our last homestand. Riske[1] just left a fastball up over the plate, and I was able to capitalize on it. What it meant to us and our standing was huge to us. They were within a game and a half, and that put us back up 2½ games. What the home run meant as far as the standings was that it was the biggest home run for me.

It's one of the best feelings a person could have. You have 20,000, 30,000 people out there cheering for you, and the game's over. It's a great feeling. It's all worth doing when you get to home plate.

I have a little girl 2 years old, Anna, and the one this year is Lucy. After the game, if you have a bad game, it doesn't matter. Every time you see them or you come off the road, they run toward you and they're yelling your name. That's stuff you just can't replace. I love being there for that.

[1] *Cleveland reliever David Riske.*

Aug. 5 at U.S. Cellular Field.

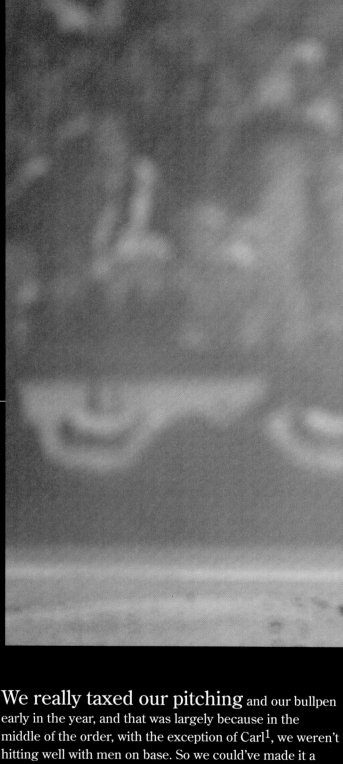

Paul Konerko

I expected us to compete and have a chance to win the division coming out of spring training because of our pitching. Then I would say from about June on, I expected the same thing I expect now. That's a chance to go deep in the postseason.

The 2000 team early in the year was a lot like this team because the pitching was going well and we could really manufacture runs. But this team was more consistent all year because our pitching didn't get hurt.

We really taxed our pitching and our bullpen early in the year, and that was largely because in the middle of the order, with the exception of Carl[1], we weren't hitting well with men on base. So we could've made it a little bit easier. So if our guys were tired at the end, it was because of how hard we worked them early on, and I take some of the blame for that because I wasn't hitting well with guys on base.

Some managers, the longer they get away

Oct. 12 in the fog after fireworks at the start of the game.

from the game, they think they're a better player. Ozzie's not like that. He just got done playing himself, and he knows the game's hard. You're going to fail a lot. He doesn't hold that against you. But if you don't work hard and play hard, he'll definitely hold that against you.

Baseball season, it's tough to step back and look at it as you're doing it every single day. But in the off-season, you look back and you're proud of what you've done. I still think there's more to come.

There's definitely your superstars— your Barry Bonds, your Alex Rodriguez. But for the rest of us, I think it's going to be what kind of important games you're playing that's going to define your career.

[1] *Carl Everett.*

Rally towels and an appetite for a postseason home victory got the crowd going for the opener of the American League Division Series on Oct. 4 against the defending champion Boston Red Sox.

The right Sox

South Siders put it all together to stun defending World Series champ Boston

By Dan McGrath

The White Sox, to paraphrase "Nuke" LaLoosh in "Bull Durham," announced their postseason presence with authority, sweeping the defending world champion Boston Red Sox out of the division series in three games.

The White Sox turned on the power in Game 1, slugging five home runs in a 14-2 rout at U.S. Cellular Field. A raucous sellout crowd of 40,717 watched the White Sox win their first postseason home game since Game 1 of the 1959 World Series. The victory-starved fans grew more appreciative in each inning, summoning Sox players for seven curtain calls over the course of the evening.

Paul Konerko got the first one, for a third-inning homer off former Cub Matt Clement. Scott Podsednik hit his first homer of the season, a three-run shot in the sixth, and A.J. Pierzynski homered twice and Juan Uribe also went deep as the White Sox doubled their scoring output from their last postseason appearance, a three-game sweep by Seattle in the 2000 division series.

Jose Contreras, meanwhile, continued his second-half dominance, limiting the hard-hitting Red Sox to two runs over $7\frac{1}{3}$ innings and retiring 14 of the final 15 hitters he faced.

The White Sox hit only one home run in Game 2, but it was a big one—a three-run shot by Tadahito Iguchi in the fifth inning that erased Boston's 4-2 lead and lifted the White Sox to a 5-4 victory.

Iguchi's blast, off former White Sox left-hander David Wells, came after former White Sox infielder Tony Graffanino failed to come up with a potential double-play grounder, extending the inning. With runners at first and third, Iguchi drove a Wells curveball into the left-field bullpen for a 5-4 lead that winning pitcher Mark Buehrle and reliever Bobby Jenks preserved.

The series shifted to Fenway Park for Game 3, a 5-3 White Sox win that turned out to be one of the most exciting games of the postseason, featuring a 58-minute sixth inning in which six pitchers threw 77 pitches.

Manny Ramirez and David Ortiz slugged back-to-back home runs for the Red Sox in the fourth inning, and, after Konerko's two-run homer had broken a 2-2 tie in the top of the sixth, Ramirez homered again.

When the Red Sox loaded the bases with nobody out against Damaso Marte, out of the bullpen came Orlando "El Duque" Hernandez, whose second-half struggles made him a controversial choice for the postseason roster. But Ozzie Guillen had a gut feeling about El Duque's big-game experience, and Hernandez rewarded his manager's faith by retiring Jason Varitek and Graffanino on popups, then striking out Johnny Damon to keep the Red Sox scoreless.

"I knew El Duque would bring cold blood," Guillen said.

After Hernandez pitched two more scoreless innings, the White Sox squeezed home an insurance run in the top of the ninth, and Jenks retired the Red Sox in order in the bottom of the ninth.

They were off to the ALCS with their first win in a postseason series since the 1917 World Series.

"El Duque earned his salary with that one inning," general manager Ken Williams said. ◆

Tadahito Iguchi's three-run blast off the pitcher White Sox fans love to beat, Boston's David Wells, put the home team ahead 5-4 in the second ALDS contest.

Frank Thomas, whose contribution to the 2005 success was powerful but brief, revs up the crowd after throwing out the first pitch of the ALDS.

Boston manager Terry Francona pulls starter and ex-Cub Matt Clement, who was pummeled by the White Sox to the tune of eight runs on seven hits, three of them homers, in Game 1.

Scott Podsednik survives a pickoff attempt and would come home
on a Paul Konerko RBI for the first run of the 14-2 rout of Boston.

High-fives all around for Tadahito Iguchi after belting a three-run shot in a five-run fifth inning that propelled the White Sox to a two-game advantage in the best-of-five series.

Joe Crede heads for third after Tony Graffanino's error on a Juan Uribe grounder set the stage for Iguchi's dramatic blast.

In the shadow
of Fenway Park's
legendary
Green Monster
left-field wall,
Game 3 starter
Freddy Garcia
and the rest
of the pitching
staff warm up
before the final
game of the
division series.

Not all fans in Wrigleyville root for the North Side team. White Sox fans go broom-crazy at Sluggers Sports Bar after the three-game sweep of the Red Sox.

Game 2 winner Mark Buehrle douses the skipper with bubbly at Fenway Park after the White Sox won their first postseason series since 1917.

The mound heroes of the ALDS clincher, closer Bobby Jenks and Orlando "El Duque" Hernandez, rejoice with their teammates.

The exuberant champs had time to savor the moment and wait for their next opponent.

American League Championship Series MVP Paul Konerko reacts to driving in an insurance run in the ninth inning of the fifth game, in which the Sox punched their ticket for the World Series with a 6-3 win.

Pitcher perfect

White Sox rotation puts on a masterful clinic to down the Angels

By Dan McGrath

One conclusion to draw from the White Sox's 4-1 victory over the Los Angeles Angels in the American League Championship Series: This team is armed and dangerous.

After spotting the Angels a 1-0 lead with their 3-2 win in Game 1, the Sox roared back with four straight complete-game pitching victories to claim the series in five games and secure their first trip to the World Series since 1959.

The Sox expected to encounter a road-weary band of Angels in the series opener. The Angels' first-round series with the New York Yankees had been delayed by rain and extended to five games, which meant the Angels had played one game in New York and another in Anaheim in the two days preceding Game 1 at U.S. Cellular Field.

But it was the Sox, coming off three days' rest, who didn't seem to have their legs under them. They scratched out just two runs against journeyman pitcher Paul Byrd and two relievers and wasted a strong effort by Jose Contreras.

Game 2 was another spine-tingling one-run affair, decided by the most bizarre play of the postseason. The teams seemed headed for extra innings when A.J. Pierzynski struck out on a Kelvim Escobar forkball to end the ninth, but umpire Doug Eddings ruled that the pitch had bounced before entering catcher Josh Paul's glove. Pierzynski ran to first as the Angels came off the field and was awarded the base on a dropped third strike.

Pablo Ozuna pinch-ran for the Sox catcher and stole second, then scored when Joe Crede lined a double into the left-field corner for a dramatic 2-1 victory, squaring the series behind Mark Buehrle's four-hit pitching.

It didn't stay squared for long. Eighteen-game winner Jon Garland made his long-awaited playoff debut in Game 3 and was nearly as effective as Buehrle, pitching a five-hitter in a 5-2 win. Paul Konerko's two-run homer keyed a three-run first inning, and the Angels never climbed out of that hole.

In Game 4 it was Freddy Garcia's turn. He went the distance on a six-hitter and Konerko hit another first-inning homer, a three-run bomb, as the Sox took command with an 8-2 win.

Contreras was back on the mound for Game 5, and it turned out to be the clincher when the Sox rallied for a 6-3 victory. Crede was the hitting star, tying the game with a seventh-inning homer off Escobar, then giving them the lead with an RBI single in the eighth. Konerko doubled in a ninth-inning insurance run, the seventh RBI of the series for the ALCS MVP.

But the story of the series was the Sox's pitching. In working $44\frac{1}{3}$ of a possible 45 innings, the starters limited the Angels to a .177 batting average and 11 runs. They had a 2.20 ERA and walked just four hitters, and Angels stars Vladimir Guerrero, Chone Figgins and Garret Anderson batted a combined .111.

"The four starters were the real horses," Konerko said. "I was just along for the ride."

A ride that would continue into the World Series. ◆

Ozzie Guillen and crew enter uncharted territory Oct. 11 at the ALCS opener.

Aaron Rowand dives for a hit off Angel Darin Erstad's bat in the seventh inning of the White Sox's 3-2 loss in the ALCS opener.

The scoreboard and the atmosphere are popping as the White Sox play for their first pennant since 1959.

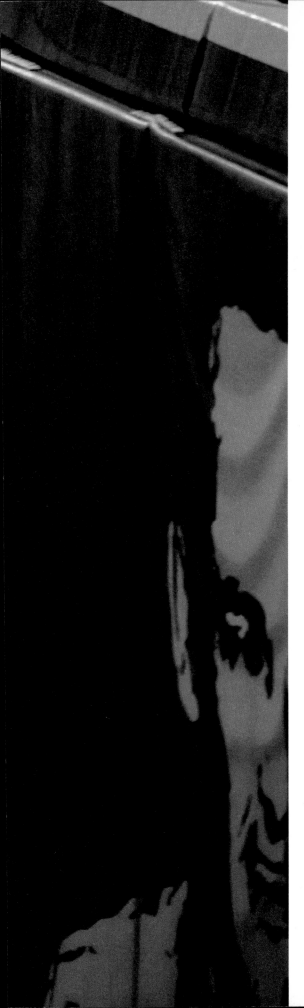

Mark Buehrle, who gave up but one run on five hits, is happy to have gotten out of a jam in Game 2. Through nine innings, he had thrown only 99 pitches and was prepared to start the 10th until his teammates won the game.

Aaron Rowand is tagged out at the plate after doubling to right and advancing to third and trying for home on Angels misplays.

Scott Podsednik grabs an Orlando Cabrera fly ball at the left-field wall to save a run with the score tied 1-1 in the seventh inning of Game 2 of the ALCS.

THE MOMENTUM SHIFT

The most controversial call of the ALCS unfolded in the bottom of the ninth in Game 2 when A.J. Pierzynski (from left, top to bottom) swung at a low pitch that was ruled to have hit the dirt. Pierzynski began to head for the dugout and then suddenly broke for first because he hadn't been tagged out by Josh Paul, the Angels' catcher. Paul rolled the ball toward the mound and was jogging back to the dugout, and Pierzynski was ruled safe at first. Arguments by Angels manager Mike Scioscia were unsuccessful.

Joe Crede rounds first after doubling in the winning run in the 2-1 victory to knot the series at a game apiece.

Paul Konerko sends a John Lackey pitch flying into the Angel Stadium seats, giving the Sox a 2-0 first-inning lead in Game 3.

Freddy Garcia celebrates the 8-2 victory after going the distance in ALCS Game 4.

Joe Crede ducks out of the way of Juan Uribe's throw to end the fourth inning of Game 4.

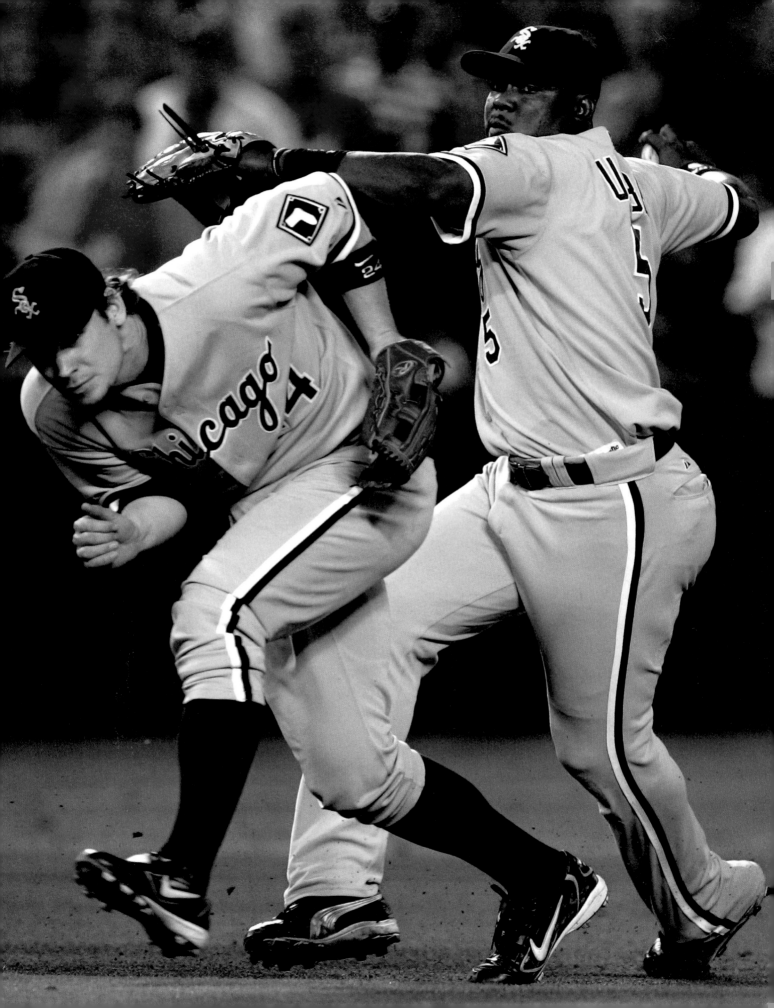

Left fielder Garret Anderson watches Paul Konerko's three-run shot sail out of the park during Game 4. It was Konerko's second consecutive game with a first-inning homer.

Mark Buehrle and teammates celebrate their Game 5 victory, bringing home the first White Sox pennant since 1959—long before Buehrle was born.

The patrons of McNally's in Sox Country at 111th and Western in Beverly rejoice in the team's ALCS championship.

Jerry Reinsdorf hoists the American League championship trophy, his first since buying the White Sox in 1981.

At last, the World Series

Chicago fans watch in disbelief as Scott Podsednik's ninth-inning fly ball sails into the right-center-field seats to give the White Sox a 7-6 victory over Houston in Game 2 of the World Series.

Autumn class

The bullpen brilliance of Neal Cotts and Bobby Jenks and Joe Crede's thrilling defense save the night

By Dan McGrath

Neither the White Sox nor their World Series opponents could be classified as hardy October perennials. The Sox hadn't been to the Series since 1959, 46 years ago, while the Houston Astros were making the first Series appearance in franchise history, a span of 44 years, or 90 combined years of classic-less falls.

That's not to say they weren't worthy.

The Sox went wire to wire in the American League Central, swept the defending champion Red Sox out of the first round in three games and needed just five to eliminate the Los Angeles Angels in the best-of-seven ALCS.

Counting the five-game winning streak with which they closed the regular season, the Sox hit the Series with 12 wins in their previous 13 games, one of their best stretches of the season.

The Astros traveled a tougher road. They lost productive veterans Jeff Kent and Carlos Beltran to free agency over the winter. Professional hitter Lance Berkman missed nearly a month because of an off-season knee injury, and veteran slugger Jeff Bagwell barely played because of a chronic shoulder problem that required surgery.

Six weeks into the season the 'Stros were limping along with a 15-30 record, and their playoff prospects were bleak at best.

But Berkman gradually regained his stroke, Morgan Ensberg had a career year, and young players Willy Taveras, Jason Lane and Mike Lamb made meaningful contributions. With Roy Oswalt, Andy Pettitte and Roger Clemens providing the league's best starting pitching and Brad Lidge doing lights-out work as the closer, Houston played .633 ball (74-43) after bottoming out at 15-30 and secured the National League's wild-card berth on the final day of the season.

The Astros needed five games to get past Atlanta in the division series, one of them an 18-inning marathon that Clemens won by pitching three innings in relief, and they beat the St. Louis Cardinals in six in the NLCS.

The forecast called for a tight World Series between similar, evenly matched teams, and the Sox's 5-3 victory in Game 1 was all of that and more.

Third baseman Joe Crede broke a 3-3 tie with a fourth-inning homer, then preserved the lead by making spectacular do-or-die fielding plays after the Astros got the potential tying run to third in the sixth and seventh innings.

In the eighth, Sox manager Ozzie Guillen went to his bullpen after Taveras led off with a double. Neal Cotts came on and gave up a single to Berkman, putting the tying run on third, but struck out Ensberg and Lamb to leave him there.

With Bagwell due up next, Guillen went for "the big boy," 270-pound rookie Bobby Jenks, who fired one blazing fastball after another at Bagwell and finally struck him out to end the inning, a classic World Series showdown and a memorable moment for the capacity crowd at U.S. Cellular Field.

Guillen let Jenks go back out to pitch the ninth, and when he gassed up and blew down Adam Everett for the final out, he and Cotts had struck out five of the seven hitters they faced in two scoreless innings.

And the Sox had made their opening statement. ◆

Closer Bobby Jenks reacts to shutting down the Houston Astros as the White Sox won the first game of the World Series 5-3.

Joe Crede sees his home run fly into the seats to give the Sox a 4-3 lead in the fourth inning of Game 1.

In the eighth inning, manager Ozzie Guillen signals to the bullpen for "the big boy," reliever Bobby Jenks, whose fastball hit 100 m.p.h. as he struck out three of the four batters he faced that night.

Catcher A.J. Pierzynski pumps his fist after Jeff Bagwell strikes out to close the eighth, leaving two runners on base.

A statue of former owner Charles Comiskey, who presided over the last White Sox world championship in 1917, is on hand with the 2005 fans as the team plays in the cold and damp of late October.

Paul Konerko rounds the bases after giving the team a 6-4 lead off a grand slam in the seventh inning.

GAME TWO: **SOX 7 ASTROS 6**

Slam-bang shocker

Game 2 was one of the more unusual White Sox games of the year, so it was fitting that it ended in highly unusual fashion.

Highly dramatic fashion, to be precise—Scott Podsednik drove ace Houston closer Brad Lidge's 2-1 pitch out to right-center field in the ninth inning for a walk-off home run that gave the Sox a 7-6 victory and a 2-0 lead in the Series before a damp, disbelieving sellout crowd at U.S. Cellular Field.

The Astros were equally incredulous—Podsednik had not hit a single home run in 507 at-bats during the regular season.

As for the White Sox … "Nobody expected that from this guy," teammate Paul Konerko said.

"Including me," Podsednik said.

Before Podsednik seized the night, Konerko struck the most telling blow. Lance Berkman had driven in three runs as the Astros took a 4-2 lead against Sox ace Mark Buehrle, but Konerko erased that deficit with one swing of his bat, greeting reliever Chad Qualls with a two-out grand slam in the seventh inning.

"I just happened to swing where he threw it," Konerko said modestly.

Konerko and Podsednik bailed out rookie reliever Bobby Jenks, who couldn't hold the 6-4 lead Konerko's slam had given him. Game 1 hero Jenks surrendered a two-run pinch single to Houston's Jose Vizcaino with two outs in the ninth.

"Bobby's one of us, and we wanted to pick him up," Konerko said.

The wave of good karma the Sox had been riding throughout the postseason was with them on the at-bat preceding Konerko's when umpire Jeff Nelson awarded Jermaine Dye first base on a pitch that appeared to hit his bat before it hit him, if in fact it hit him. Dye later acknowledged that it hadn't.

"They can't do anything wrong right now," Astros manager Phil Garner said enviously.

On an otherwise damp and dreary night at the Cell, it was hard to argue with him. ◆

Chris Burke beats the tag to tie the score in the top of the ninth inning of Game 2, setting the stage for Scott Podsednik's bottom-of-the-ninth drama.

Larry Robinson cheers on the White Sox during the game while doing his laundry at the Spin Cycle laundromat on the Southwest Side.

Scott Podsednik tracks his walk-off homer in the 7-6 victory.

Game 2 hero Scott Podsednik is swarmed by his teammates after belting a game-winning homer in the bottom of the ninth to give the Sox a 7-6 victory and a 2-0 World Series lead.

An Astros fan hopes a voodoo doll will work magic against the Sox in Game 3. It didn't.

GAME THREE: **SOX 7 ASTROS 5**

A late bloomer

If Scott Podsednik was an unlikely long-ball hero in Game 2, how about Geoff Blum in Game 3? How do you believe it's anything but your year when the probable 25th man on your roster hits a home run to decide the longest World Series game ever played in your favor?

That was the scenario when Blum stepped to the plate to face Ezequiel Astacio in the wee hours of a Wednesday morning, five hours, 41 minutes and 14 innings after Podsednik had stepped in against Houston's Roy Oswalt to get Game 3 under way at Minute Maid Park. White Sox manager Ozzie Guillen had exhausted his roster, and Astacio was the 16th of 17 pitchers who would be used.

Blum, a former Astro acquired from San Diego at the trading deadline, was batting for the first time in a World Series. He got a 2-0 pitch to his liking and ripped it into the stands down the right-field line to break a stubborn 5-5 tie that had existed since the eighth inning. Astacio then walked in another run as the Sox won 7-5 to take a 3-0 lead in the Series and add a sense of urgency to the plans for a victory celebration taking shape back in Chicago.

Blum had to laugh when he was asked if the home run was the biggest hit of his modest journeyman's career.

"A home run to win a World Series game in extra innings—are you kidding me?" he said. "I've done it or dreamed about it thousands of times in the back yard playing wiffle ball with my brother, but to do it for real ... there's no words to describe it."

The Sox sent 11 men to the plate and scored five runs off Oswalt in the fifth inning, but the Astros tied it in the eighth, and neither team could dent the other's bullpen until Blum did so the next day. Guillen even ran out of relievers and called upon Mark Buehrle to get the final out.

Blum's wife had given birth to triplets earlier in the season. "Nothing can ever top that, but as far as thrills go, this is comparable," he said.

White Sox fans probably would agree. ◆

Joe Crede rounds the bases after homering to start a five-run fifth-inning comeback that saw the Sox go ahead by 1.

An Astros fan sports a Texas-sized foam hat for Game 3.

The Sox used nine pitchers in the longest game in World Series history, the 14-inning, 5-hour, 41-minute Game 3. Starter Jon Garland (from left, top) was followed by Cliff Politte, Neal Cotts, Dustin Hermanson, Orlando Hernandez, Jose Vizcaino, Bobby Jenks and Damaso Marte before Mark Buehrle closed it out at 1:20 a.m.

Geoff Blum is congratulated for breaking the 5-5 deadlock in the 14th inning with a solo homer. Blum had not played since the first game of the playoffs.

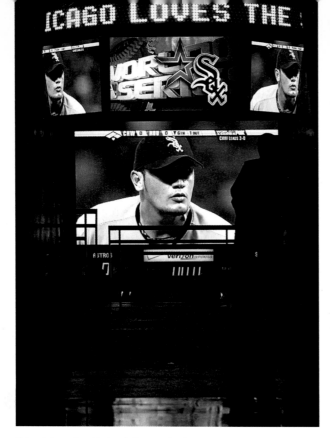

Watching the United Center's giant projection screens surrounded by thousands of White Sox fans: $15. Seeing your beloved team win the World Series: priceless.

GAME FOUR: **SOX 1 ASTROS 0**

Bringing it home

White Sox shortstop Juan Uribe played all 14 innings of the 5-hour, 41-minute Game 3 marathon the night before, yet he was frisky as a kitten in the ninth inning of Game 4.

With the Sox leading 1-0 and the tying run at second base, Uribe literally ran into the stands down the line from third base to catch a foul pop off the bat of Chris Burke, retiring him for the second out.

Pinch-hitter Orlando Palmeiro then hit a slow chopper past the mound, and Uribe dashed in to glove it and nail Palmeiro at first with a strong throw.

Just like that, the White Sox were world champions. Their on-field celebration was spontaneous, exuberant and long overdue—88 years had passed since their last World Series title, and seven had passed since a Chicago team, the Bulls, had hoisted a championship banner.

Sox fans from Bourbonnais to Barrington joined in the party vicariously, as did the few hundred who had made their way to Minute Maid Park in anticipation of just such a moment. After watching so many fans in so many other cities celebrate so often, it was almost as if they didn't know what to do with themselves besides smile, shout and hug somebody.

"A lot of people have waited a long time for this, and I'm glad we were able to give it to them," Sox manager Ozzie Guillen said.

Freddy Garcia and three relievers combined on a five-hitter, but Houston's Brandon Backe was every bit their equal in his seven shutout innings. The Sox finally "small-balled" their way to the game's only run in the eighth, when Series MVP Jermaine Dye singled home Willie Harris, who had reached on a pinch single and moved around on a sacrifice bunt and a groundout.

The formula the Sox devised in spring training—strong pitching, tight defense and clubhouse togetherness—was followed to the letter during a 99-win regular season and one of the most dominant playoff runs in recent memory. The Sox

went 11-1 in the postseason, taking care of the Boston Red Sox, the Los Angeles Angels and the Astros as their starting pitchers gave them at least seven innings in 11 of the 12 games.

And the White Sox are world champions.

"I didn't come here for the glamor, I didn't come here for the money. I came here to win," Guillen said.

Mission accomplished. ◆

Joe Crede, Scott Podsednik and countless fans on the third-base line watch in amazement as Juan Uribe snatches a foul pop in the ninth inning. The sensational play left the White Sox one out away from the title.

Manager Ozzie Guillen crosses a sea of photographers as he carries the World Series trophy out onto the field after the White Sox's four-game sweep of the Houston Astros.

Carl Everett carries Willie Harris around the field during the celebration. Every player on the White Sox roster saw some action during the team's championship run.

Fans cheer and wave brooms outside U.S. Cellular Field, a logical gathering place to celebrate a World Series championship on a night that will long be remembered by many Chicagoans.

Halsted Street at 35th is the setting for an impromptu victory parade after the clincher.

Let the party begin. The White Sox celebrate on the field in Houston what they began last winter in Tucson.

White Sox chairman Jerry Reinsdorf is surrounded by his team, staff and their families as he clutches the World Series trophy, a prize that has not made its home in Chicago in 88 years.

YEAR	WON	LOST	WINNING PCT.	PLACE	QUICK HIT
1901	83	53	.610	1	Sox champs in AL's first year behind Clark Griffith (24-7) and Fielder Jones (.340).
1902	74	60	.552	4	Sox finish 8 behind in Griffith's second and last year as player-manager.
1903	60	77	.438	7	Newcomer Doc White (17-6, 2.13 ERA) lone bright spot as team winds up 30½ back.
1904	89	65	.578	3	Fielder Jones takes over as manager in May; team goes 66-47 rest of way.
1905	92	60	.605	2	Nick Altrock, Frank Owen both win 20-plus as Sox finish 2 behind champion A's.
1906	**93**	**58**	**.616**	**1**	"Hitless Wonders" post AL lows in batting (.230) and homers (7) but win pennant.
					WORLD SERIES: Beat favored Cubs 4 games to 2 in World Series, allowing 10 earned runs, 27 hits.
1907	87	64	.576	3	Finish 5½ out despite Doc White (27-13) and Ed Walsh (1.60 ERA, 422 ⅓ innings).
1908	88	64	.579	3	Walsh goes 40-15 with 1.42 ERA but Sox lose to Detroit and Ty Cobb by 1½ games.
1909	78	74	.513	4	Drop to 20½ games back; Frank Smith (24-17), Walsh (1.41) the leaders.
1910	68	85	.444	6	Highlight is July 1 opening of 30,000-seat Comiskey Park at 35th and Wentworth.
1911	77	74	.510	4	Matty McIntyre hits .323, Ping Bodie drives in 97 runs, Walsh wins 27.
1912	78	76	.506	4	Big Ed Walsh's last big year: 27-12, 2.15 ERA, 254 strikeouts in 393 innings.
1913	78	74	.513	5	2nd-year SS Buck Weaver's 52 RBIs leads team; Eddie Cicotte 18-12, 1.58.
1914	70	84	.455	6	Team's collapse—30 games out of 1st place—costs manager Nixie Callahan his job.
1915	93	61	.604	3	Joe Jackson comes from Cleveland in Aug. 21 deal for 3 players, $31,500.
1916	89	65	.578	2	2nd-year manager Pants Rowland gets Sox closer to pennant goal: 2 games behind Boston.
1917	**100**	**54**	**.649**	**1**	Cicotte (28-12, 1.53) and Happy Felsch (.308, 102 RBIs) power pennant push.
					WORLD SERIES: Eddie Collins (.409), Weaver (.333) and Red Faber (3 wins) help stop NY Giants in 6.
1918	57	67	.460	6	World War I takes toll on Sox's record and home attendance (195,081).
1919	**88**	**52**	**.629**	**1**	Jackson (.351, 96 RBIs) and Cicotte (29-7, 1.82) help Sox beat out Cleveland by 3½.
					WORLD SERIES: Heavily favored Sox lose to Reds 5 games to 3; not long thereafter, we learn why.
1920	96	58	.623	2	Greatest Sox team ever? Collins (.372), Jackson (.382, 121 RBIs), four 20-game winners.
1921	62	92	.403	7	Minus 8 banned "Black Sox," Sox tumble into 2nd division and stay there till 1936.
1922	77	77	.500	5	Highlight is Charley Robertson's perfect game on April 30 against Detroit.
1923	69	85	.448	7	Plummet to 30 games back despite more heroics by Collins (.360, 47 steals).
1924	66	87	.431	8	Club hits bottom despite Bibb Falk (.352) and 20-game winner Hollis Thurston, later top Sox scout.
1925	79	75	.513	5	Ted Lyons (21-11), just out of Baylor University, enjoys first big season.
1926	81	72	.529	5	Falk (.345, 108 RBIs) and CF Johnny Mostil (.328, 35 steals) keys to improvement.
1927	70	83	.458	5	Lyons (22-14, 2.84 ERA, 307 innings) is among the few bright spots.
1928	72	82	.468	5	New 3B Willie Kamm arrives from Pacific Coast League and hits .308 with 84 RBIs.
1929	59	93	.388	7	Manager Lena Blackburne gets punched out by rookie 1B Art Shires. Both lose their jobs.
1930	62	92	.403	7	New manager Donie Bush isn't the answer: Sox finish 40 games out.
1931	56	97	.366	8	Carl Reynolds goes from 22 homers to 6; Sox finish 51½ games behind.
1932	49	102	.325	7	Under new manager Lew Fonseca, Sox draw 233,198 and end up 56½ back.
1933	67	83	.447	7	Sox buy A's greats Al Simmons, Mule Haas and Jimmy Dykes; they don't help much.
1934	53	99	.349	8	Dykes takes over as manager; rookie 1B Zeke Bonura has 27 homers, 110 RBIs.
1935	74	78	.487	5	Drive toward respectability continues behind Luke Appling (.307), Bonura, Lyons.
1936	81	70	.536	3	Eureka! Sox reach 1st division as Appling (.388) wins batting title, Bonura collects 138 RBIs.
1937	86	68	.558	3	Heroes are Bonura (.345, 19 homers, 100 RBIs) and Monte Stratton (15-5, 2.40 ERA).
1938	65	83	.439	6	Broken ankle sidelines Appling 73 games; Stratton goes 15-9 but winter gun accident ends career.
1939	85	69	.552	4	Johnny Rigney beats Browns in Comiskey Park's first night game Aug. 14.
1940	82	72	.532	4	Trail 1st-place Cleveland by 4 games Sept. 15 before going into 3-7 tailspin.
1941	77	77	.500	3	Taffy Wright bats .322, Appling hits .314 and Lee goes 22-11 with 2.37 ERA.
1942	66	82	.446	6	Sox start off 4-18, and things don't get much better. Lyons wins 20 games, all on Sundays.
1943	82	72	.532	4	Sox move back into 1st division with many players starting to go off to war.
1944	71	83	.461	7	Appling goes into the military, and with him goes any hope of respectablity.
1945	71	78	.477	6	The final war year. 3B Tony Cuccinello hits .308 and loses the batting title by 1 point!
1946	74	80	.481	5	Dykes, after 12-plus years, is fired as manager in late May. Lyons takes over.
1947	70	84	.455	6	Appling leads club with a .306 average and is given a new car on June 8, "Luke Appling Day."
1948	51	101	.336	8	Fat Pat Seerey's 4-homer day in Philadelphia is among the few highlights.
1949	63	91	.409	6	New GM Frank Lane's 1st acquisition, pitcher Billy Pierce (age 22), goes 7-15 with 3.88 ERA.
1950	60	94	.390	6	Pierce wins 12, rookie SS Chico Carrasquel is sensational and 2B Nellie Fox shows promise.
1951	81	73	.526	4	New manager Paul Richards has "Go-Go Sox" in 1st on July 4. New stars: Minnie Minoso and Jim Busby.
1952	81	73	.526	3	Minoso, Fox fall off '51 pace but club rises to 3rd thanks in part to Pierce (15-12, 2.57).
1953	89	65	.578	3	Pierce (18-12), Virgil Trucks (20-10) and Minoso (.313, 104 RBIs) keys to best mark since 1920.
1954	94	60	.610	3	Injuries to Pierce, 1B Ferris Fain and 3B George Kell ruin a potential pennant season.
1955	91	63	.591	3	Sox lead AL heading into Labor Day weekend but fade. Dick Donovan's appendectomy doesn't help.
1956	85	69	.552	3	Larry Doby adds power (24 HRs, 102 RBIs), Pierce wins 20 and SS Luis Aparicio is AL's top rookie.
1957	90	64	.584	2	New manager Al Lopez has Sox 6 games ahead of Yankees in June. Pierce wins 20 again.
1958	82	72	.532	2	A lost season, but trades bring key '59 components. Bill Veeck buys control in December.
1959	**94**	**60**	**.610**	**1**	Sox, 35-15 in 1-run games, clinch pennant Sept. 22 at Cleveland. Early Wynn goes 22-10.
					WORLD SERIES: After 11-0 Game 1 rout of Dodgers, Sox score 12 runs rest of way and lose Series 4 games to 2.
1960	87	67	.565	3	Sox 2 games back with 2½ weeks left, but Yankees closed season with 15-game win streak.
1961	86	76	.531	4	After horrible start, Sox win 19 of 20 in June to regain respectability. Veeck sells club in June.
1962	85	77	.525	5	Ray Herbert wins 20 games for new-look club that had traded old favorites Pierce and Minoso.
1963	94	68	.580	2	Aparicio trade brings Pete Ward, Ron Hansen and Hoyt Wilhelm. Sox climb back into contention.

White Sox pitcher Eddie Cicotte hands a ball to his wife and daughter at a game celebrating Military Day during the championship 1917 season.

Jubilant fans hail their White Sox as they land at Midway Airport after capturing the 1959 American League pennant with a victory in Cleveland.

YEAR	WON	LOST	WINNING PCT.	PLACE	QUICK HIT
1964	98	64	.605	2	Losing first 10 meetings to New York especially hurts when Sox finish 1 game behind Yankees.
1965	95	67	.586	2	Injuries to lefties Gary Peters and Juan Pizarro hamper efforts to catch Minnesota.
1966	83	79	.512	4	Strong 2nd half saves new manager Eddie Stanky. CF Tommie Agee is AL rookie of the year.
1967	89	73	.549	4	Sox blow final 5 games (to weaklings Kansas City and Washington) and lose pennant they should have won.
1968	67	95	.414	8	Sox regain Aparicio and trade for NL star Tommy Davis but lose first 10 games of season—and all hope.
1969	68	94	.420	5	Only positive the play of youngsters Carlos May, Bill Melton and Walter Williams.
1970	56	106	.346	6	September shakeup brings GM Roland Hemond, manager Chuck Tanner, pitching coach Johnny Sain.
1971	79	83	.488	3	Converted reliever Wilbur Wood wins 22 games, Melton lands AL homer title with 33.
1972	87	67	.565	2	New 1B Dick Allen wins MVP award (37 homers, .308) as Sox fight world champ Oakland to the wire.
1973	77	85	.475	5	Sox lead AL West by 5 games in late May before injuries (CF Ken Henderson, Allen) wreck season.
1974	80	80	.500	4	Addition of Ron Santo from Cubs is of no help. Allen announces retirement in September.
1975	75	86	.466	5	Club's poor showing on field and at gate lead to John Allyn's sale of Sox to Bill Veeck in fall.
1976	64	97	.398	6	Paul Richards, managing again at 67, leads Sox to 27-22 record in early June before reality hits.
1977	90	72	.556	3	Veeck's South Side Hit Men homer their way into AL West lead before Kansas City takes charge.
1978	71	90	.441	5	Sox can't replace Richie Zisk and Oscar Gamble. Manager Bob Lemon is let go in June.
1979	73	87	.456	5	Tony La Russa replaces Don Kessinger as manager in August; Sox go 27-27 thereafter.
1980	70	90	.438	5	Unveiled are pitching prospects Britt Burns and Richard Dotson and rookie RF Harold Baines.
1981	54	52	.509		In strike-interrupted season, respectability returns in veterans Carlton Fisk and Greg Luzinski.
1982	87	75	.537	3	Sox show progress and, in September, show off call-ups Ron Kittle and Greg Walker.
1983	99	63	.611	1	Kittle hits 35 homers, Luzinski 32; LaMarr Hoyt wins 24, Dotson 22; Fisk has MVP-type season.
					ALCS: Sox win opener 2-1 in Baltimore but score one run in next three games.
1984	74	88	.457	5	Sox lead weak AL West with 44-40 mark at All-Star break and then totally collapse.
1985	85	77	.525	3	SS Ozzie Guillen is AL rookie of the year, Tom Seaver wins his 300th and Fisk hits 37 homers.
1986	72	90	.444	5	TV's "Hawk" Harrelson becomes GM, trades liberally, fires La Russa and, at season's end, flees the scene.
1987	77	85	.475	5	Best development of this season is the drafting of Jack McDowell, right-hander from Stanford.
1988	71	90	.441	5	On June 30, the General Assembly passes legislation for a new stadium, keeping the Sox in Chicago.
1989	69	92	.429	7	Sox, under Jeff Torborg, close with 38-37 "run" and kids Sammy Sosa and Robin Ventura in lineup.
1990	94	68	.580	2	Old Comiskey's swan song memorable, thanks to Fisk, Sosa, Ventura and a young Frank Thomas.
1991	87	75	.537	2	New Comiskey opens, Thomas and Ventura blossom, but an August skid ends pennant hopes.
1992	86	76	.531	3	Knee injury to Guillen in season's 13th game makes for lost season. Thomas hits .323 with 115 RBIs.
1993	94	68	.580	1	McDowell, Alex Fernandez, Wilson Alvarez and Jason Bere-a rotation to remember.
					ALCS: Sox drop all three home playoff games and fall to world champion Toronto 4 games to 2.
1994	67	46	.593	1	Strike-shortened season costs Sox shot at World Series. Thomas has 38 homers, 101 RBIs in 113 games.
1995	68	76	.472	3	Judge orders players back to work in late April, but Sox never appear ready.
1996	85	77	.525	2	Lead wild-card race by 3½ games in mid-August but lose 11 of next 20.
1997	80	81	.497	2	Trailing Cleveland by 3½ games on July 30, Sox pull trigger on "White Flag" trade with Giants.
1998	80	82	.494	2	A lost season, except for Albert Belle: 49 homers, 152 RBIs and .328 average.
1999	75	86	.466	2	Another lost year, save for Magglio Ordoñez's coming-out party: .301 average, 30 homers, 117 RBIs.
2000	95	67	.586	1	Thomas' last great year propels Sox to AL Central title: .328, 43 homers, 143 RBIs.
					ALDS: Unhealthy pitching staff and poor clutch hitting keys to Sox's being swept three straight by Seattle.
2001	83	79	.512	3	Season-ending injury to Thomas in late April contributes mightily to Sox's nosedive.
2002	81	81	.500	2	Bright spots include the play of Ordoñez (.320, 38 homers, 135 RBIs) and Mark Buehrle (19-12, 3.58).
2003	86	76	.531	2	Win first 2 games of Sept. home series vs. Twins, lose final 2 and are swept 3 in Minneapolis the next week.
2004	83	79	.512	2	Season-ending injuries to Thomas and Ordoñez make for a trying managerial debut for Ozzie Guillen
2005	99	63	.611	1	A 15-game AL Central lead slips to 1½ before Sox take charge in final week.
					ALDS: Home runs throughout and clutch relief work by Orlando Hernandez in Game 3 help Sox sweep Boston.
					ALCS: Paul Konerko's home runs, Joe Crede's clutch hitting and brilliant starting pitching oust the Angels in 5.
					WORLD SERIES: Dominant playoff run continues with sweep of Astros in four close games.

Note: 8-club league through 1960; 10-club league 1961-68; two 6-club divisions 1969-1976; two 7-club divisions 1977-1993; three divisions 1994 to present.

2005 roster

GS	CG	IP	SV	P/IP	BAA	WHIP	ERA
Games started	Complete games	Innings pitched	Saves	Pitches per inning pitched	Batting average against	Walks+hits per inning pitched	Earned-run average

MARK BUEHRLE
Pitcher
Bats: Left Throws: Left
Height: 6-2 Weight: 220
Age: 26 ML Exp.: 6 yrs.

56

	G	GS	CG	IP	H	R	ER	HR	BB	SO	W	L	SV	P/IP	BAA	WHIP	ERA
Season	33	33	3	236.2	240	99	82	20	40	149	16	8	0	14.70	.262	1.18	3.12
Playoffs	4	3	1	23.1	20	9	9	2	1	12	2	0	1	12.73	0.23	0.90	3.47
Career	197	172	18	1,224	1,226	560	494	129	730	730	85	53	0	15.05	.262	1.23	3.6

Still considered the elder statesman of the pitching staff, he started and won the All-Star Game. Showed his toughness by coming in to finish Game 3 against Houston and earn a save.

FREDDY GARCIA
Pitcher
Bats: Right Throws: Right
Height: 6-4 Weight: 250
Age: 29 ML Exp.: 7 yrs.

34

	G	GS	CG	IP	H	R	ER	HR	BB	SO	W	L	SV	P/IP	BAA	WHIP	ER
Season	33	33	2	228	225	102	98	26	60	146	14	8	0	14.90	.259	1.25	3.8
Playoffs	3	3	1	21	15	5	5	3	8	13	3	0	0	15.29	.205	1.10	2.1
Career	219	218	11	1,427.1	1,356	659	623	159	481	1067	99	62	0	15.94	.249	1.29	3.9

Won only 14 games but finished 10-3 on the road compared to 4-5 at U.S. Cellular Field. Threw a one-hitter against the Twins and still lost 1-0 on a home run.

JON GARLAND
Pitcher
Bats: Right Throws: Right
Height: 6-6 Weight: 215
Age: 26 ML Exp.: 6 yrs.

20

	G	GS	CG	IP	H	R	ER	HR	BB	SO	W	L	SV	P/IP	BAA	WHIP	ERA
Season	32	32	3	221	212	93	86	26	47	115	18	10	0	15.00	.255	1.17	3.5
Playoffs	2	2	1	16	11	6	4	2	3	11	1	0	0	13.19	.208	0.88	2.2
Career	181	159	5	1,009	1,016	544	496	137	551	551	64	61	1	15.98	.265	1.38	4.4

Enjoyed a breakout season with 18 victories and three shutouts. Named to the All-Star team for his 13-4 record in the first half, including eight victories before losing his first game.

JOSE CONTRERAS
Pitcher
Bats: Right Throws: Right
Height: 6-4 Weight: 245
Age: 33 ML Exp.: 3 yrs.

52

	G	GS	CG	IP	H	R	ER	HR	BB	SO	W	L	SV	P/IP	BAA	WHIP	ERA
Season	32	32	1	204.2	177	91	82	23	75	154	15	7	0	15.48	.232	1.23	3.6
Playoffs	4	4	1	32	26	11	11	2	2	14	3	1	0	12.44	0.222	0.88	3.0
Career	81	72	1	446	395	232	212	58	376	376	35	18	0	16.35	.236	1.31	4.2

Turned around his career in the second half of the season while compiling a 6-0 record and 1.99 ERA in September. He established career highs with 15 victories, 204²/₃ innings and 154 strikeouts after languishing with Yankees.

ORLANDO HERNANDEZ
Pitcher
Bats: Right Throws: Right
Height: 6-2 Weight: 220
Age: 36 ML Exp.: 7 yrs.

26

	G	GS	CG	IP	H	R	ER	HR	BB	SO	W	L	SV	P/IP	BAA	WHIP	ER
Season	24	22	0	128.1	137	77	73	18	50	91	9	9	1	17.52	.275	1.46	5.1
Playoffs	2	0	0	4	1	0	0	0	4	6	0	0	0	19.25	.077	1.25	0.0
Career	163	158	8	1,004.2	917	487	459	132	354	794	70	49	2	—	.242	1.27	4.1

Signed late in the off-season, Hernandez won nine games and proved his veteran value when he escaped two bases-loaded jams as a reliever in the playoffs. Also helped turn around the career of Contreras with his mentoring.

LUIS VIZCAINO
Pitcher
Bats: Right Throws: Right
Height: 5-11 Weight: 185
Age: 31 ML Exp.: 7 yrs.

51

	G	GS	CG	IP	H	R	ER	HR	BB	SO	W	L	SV	P/IP	BAA	WHIP	ER
Season	65	0	0	70	74	30	29	8	29	43	6	5	0	16.63	.275	1.47	3.7
Playoffs	1	0	0	1	0	0	0	0	1	0	0	0	0	14.00	.000	1.00	0.0
Career	338	0	0	344.2	320	175	167	53	134	297	21	17	7	16.66	.245	1.32	4.3

Acquired in off-season trade with Milwaukee, Vizcaino won six games while making 65 relief appearances. He posted 2.60 ERA after the All-Star break but blew all three of his save chances.

CLIFF POLITTE
Pitcher
Bats: Right Throws: Right
Height: 5-10 Weight: 200
Age: 31 ML Exp.: 8 yrs.

18

	G	GS	CG	IP	H	R	ER	HR	BB	SO	W	L	SV	P/IP	BAA	WHIP	ER
Season	68	0	0	67.1	42	15	15	7	21	57	7	1	1	15.12	.181	0.94	2.0
Playoffs	4	0	0	3.1	1	1	1	0	2	2	0	0	00	14.70	.091	0.90	2.7
Career	300	16	0	381.1	346	184	172	47	327	327	20	21	15	—	.242	1.32	4.0

Probably most surprising and overlooked season of all, Politte finished 7-1 while becoming the main right-handed setup man. Ranked second in the AL in fewest hits allowed per nine innings and fourth in opponents' batting average.

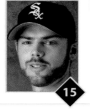

L TTS

 her

: Left **Throws:** Left

ght: 6-2 **Weight:** 205

: 25 **ML Exp.:** 3 yrs.

	G	GS	CG	IP	H	R	ER	HR	BB	SO	W	L	SV	P/IP	BAA	WHIP	ERA
Season	69	0	0	60.1	38	15	13	1	29	58	4	0	0	16.56	.179	1.11	1.94
Playoffs	6	0	0	2.1	1	0	0	0	1	2	1	0	0	18.00	.125	0.86	0.00
Career	129	5	0	139	114	72	66	15	76	126	9	5	0	17.99	.224	1.37	4.27

He took over the left-handed setup role and led the league for relievers in fewest homers per nine innings and was second in retiring the first batter he faced. After his first three outings, he compiled a 1.59 ERA for rest of the season.

TIN RMANSON

her

: Right **Throws:** Right

ght: 6-2 **Weight:** 200

: 32 **ML Exp.:** 11 yrs.

	G	GS	CG	IP	H	R	ER	HR	BB	SO	W	L	SV	P/IP	BAA	WHIP	ERA
Season	57	0	0	57.1	46	17	13	4	17	33	2	4	34	14.51	.222	1.10	2.04
Playoffs	1	0	0	0.1	1	0	0	0	0	1	0	0	0	24.00	.500	3.00	0.00
Career	351	180	4	1,276.1	1,279	672	597	158	459	869	73	78	56	—	.263	1.36	4.21

Before he was slowed by back problems, Hermanson saved his first 15 games and had 21 by the All-Star break. The former starter was signed for the bullpen as a free agent and was an immediate success.

MASO RTE

her

: Left **Throws:** Left

ght: 6-2 **Weight:** 205

: 30 **ML Exp.:** 6 yrs.

	G	GS	CG	IP	H	R	ER	HR	BB	SO	W	L	SV	P/IP	BAA	WHIP	ERA
Season	66	0	0	45.1	45	21	19	5	33	54	3	4	4	19.99	.256	1.72	3.77
Playoffs	2	0	0	1.2	1	0	0	0	4	3	0	0	0	33	.143	3.00	0.00
Career	307	0	0	304	245	114	108	31	137	323	14	14	31	17.14	.223	1.26	3.2

Inadvertently, he helped bring the team together late in the season when he left after a spat with manager Ozzie Guillen. Saved four games and was the winning pitcher in Game 3 of the World Series against Houston.

BY NKS

her

: Right **Throws:** Right

ght: 6-3 **Weight:** 270

: 24 **ML Exp.:** 1 yr.

	G	GS	CG	IP	H	R	ER	HR	BB	SO	W	L	SV	P/IP	BAA	WHIP	ERA
Season	32	0	0	39.1	34	15	12	3	15	50	1	1	6	16.50	.225	1.25	2.75
Playoffs	6	0	0	8	4	2	2	0	3	8	0	0	4	16.13	.148	0.88	2.25
Career	32	0	0	39.1	34	15	12	3	15	50	1	1	6	16.50	.225	1.25	2.75

Became a late-season success story with his 100 m.p.h. fastball after starting at Double A. He averaged 11.44 strikeouts per nine innings while saving six games and saving Sox after Hermanson was limited.

TTING

CS	AVG	OBP	SLG	OPS
ht stealing	Batting average	On-base percentage	Slugging percentage	On-base percentage + slugging percentage

RON WAND

ter field

: Right **Throws:** Right

ght: 6-0 **Weight:** 200

: 28 **ML Exp.:** 5 yrs.

	G	AB	R	H	2B	3B	HR	RBI	TB	BB	SO	SB	CS	OBP	SLG	OPS	AVG
Season	157	578	77	156	30	5	13	69	235	32	116	16	5	.329	.407	.736	.270
Playoffs	12	45	8	12	6	0	0	3	18	4	9	1	0	.333	.400	.733	.267
Career	579	1,647	255	466	97	9	54	211	743	96	310	38	12	.337	.451	.788	.283

Was Gold Glove caliber in center field and the personification of toughness while being hit by pitches 21 times, second most in Sox history. He established career high in hits and matched his high in RBI.

L NERKO

base

: Right **Throws:** Right

ght: 6-2 **Weight:** 215

: 29 **ML Exp.:** 9 yrs.

	G	AB	R	H	2B	3B	HR	RBI	TB	BB	SO	SB	CS	OBP	SLG	OPS	AVG
Season	158	575	98	163	24	0	40	100	307	81	109	0	0	.375	.534	.909	.283
Playoffs	12	49	6	13	2	0	5	15	30	3	8	0	0	.321	.612	.933	.265
Career	1,123	3,995	580	1,115	196	5	210	692	1,951	400	609	4	1	.349	.488	.837	.279

Cemented his position as one of top power hitters in baseball with a second consecutive 40-homer, 100-RBI season. He also served as unofficial team spokesman, a soothing voice of reason during even the toughest of times.

MAINE E

t field

: Right **Throws:** Right

ght: 6-5 **Weight:** 220

: 31 **ML Exp.:** 10 yrs.

	G	AB	R	H	2B	3B	HR	RBI	TB	BB	SO	SB	CS	OBP	SLG	OPS	AVG
Season	145	529	74	145	29	2	31	86	271	39	99	11	4	.333	.512	.846	.274
Playoffs	12	45	7	14	3	0	1	6	20	6	7	1	0	.415	.444	.860	.311
Career	1,184	4,347	639	1,182	242	19	192	697	2,038	385	871	34	18	.334	.469	.803	.272

Quietly effective, his burden of replacing popular Magglio Ordoñez was heavy.
He hit 31 home runs and led Sox outfielders with nine assists.

TADAHITO IGUCHI

Second base
Bats: Right **Throws:** Right
Height: 5-10 **Weight:** 185
Age: 30 **ML Exp.:** 1yr.

	G	AB	R	H	2B	3B	HR	RBI	TB	BB	SO	SB	CS	OBP	SLG	OPS	AV
Season	135	511	74	142	25	6	15	71	224	47	114	15	5	.342	.438	.780	.27
Playoffs	12	47	7	9	1	0	1	5	13	2	12	0	1	.269	.277	.546	.19
Career	135	511	74	142	25	6	15	71	224	47	114	15	5	.342	.438	.780	.27

Last-minute addition from Japan was called team MVP for much of season. His transition from power producer to No. 2 hitter was immediate, as he helped Podsednik set the table.

SCOTT PODSEDNIK

Center Field
Bats: Left **Throws:** Left
Height: 6-0 **Weight:** 190
Age: 29 **ML Exp.:** 5 yrs.

	G	AB	R	H	2B	3B	HR	RBI	TB	BB	SO	SB	CS	OBP	SLG	OPS	AV
Season	129	507	80	147	28	1	0	25	177	47	75	59	23	.351	.349	.700	.29
Playoffs	12	49	9	14	1	3	2	6	27	7	10	6	3	.397	.551	.948	.28
Career	456	1,731	268	483	84	17	22	130	667	165	278	172	46	.345	.385	.730	.27

Became the face of the small-ball mentality with his speed from the leadoff spot. He was a huge reason Sox outscored opponents 121-68 in the first inning.

CARL EVERETT

Right Field
Bats: Switch **Throws:** Right
Height: 6-0 **Weight:** 215
Age: 34 **ML Exp.:** 13 yrs.

	G	AB	R	H	2B	3B	HR	RBI	TB	BB	SO	SB	CS	OBP	SLG	OPS	AV
Season	135	490	58	123	17	2	23	87	213	42	99	4	5	.311	.435	.745	.25
Playoffs	12	40	5	12	0	0	0	3	12	1	6	0	1	.333	.300	.633	.30
Career	1,313	4,501	670	1,234	250	26	191	759	2,109	413	964	106	51	.344	.469	.812	.27

Despite his different ways, Everett became more valuable when Frank Thomas missed most of the season. He averaged one RBI every 5.63 at-bats, the 12th-best figure in the American League.

JUAN URIBE

Short stop
Bats: Right **Throws:** Right
Height: 5-11 **Weight:** 215
Age: 26 **ML Exp.:** 5 yrs.

	G	AB	R	H	2B	3B	HR	RBI	TB	BB	SO	SB	CS	OBP	SLG	OPS	AV
Season	146	481	58	121	23	3	16	71	198	34	77	4	6	.301	.412	.712	.25
Playoffs	12	42	7	12	5	0	1	6	20	5	8	1	0	.362	.476	.838	.28
Career	594	2,138	286	561	113	30	63	280	923	125	408	32	21	.305	.432	.737	.26

His emergence as sure-handed everyday shortstop was one of the keys to the seasons. His 40 RBIs, including 10 on sacrifice flies, from the ninth position tied for best in baseball.

A.J. PIERZYNSKI

Catcher
Bats: Left **Throws:** Left
Height: 6-3 **Weight:** 240
Age: 28 **ML Exp.:** 8 yrs.

	G	AB	R	H	2B	3B	HR	RBI	TB	BB	SO	SB	CS	OBP	SLG	OPS	AV
Season	128	460	61	118	21	0	18	56	193	23	68	0	2	.308	.420	.728	.2
Playoffs	12	42	9	11	4	0	3	9	24	4	8	2	1	.340	.400	.912	.2
Career	689	2,359	290	676	155	14	55	326	1,024	102	288	6	13	.330	.434	.765	.2

Rewarded the Sox for taking a chance on his reputation and emerged as one of the popular team leaders. Hit a career-high 18 home runs and led all AL catchers in fielding percentage.

JOE CREDE

Third base
Bats: Right **Throws:** Right
Height: 6-1 **Weight:** 195
Age: 27 **ML Exp.:** 6 yrs.

	G	AB	R	H	2B	3B	HR	RBI	TB	BB	SO	SB	CS	OBP	SLG	OPS	AV
Season	132	432	54	109	21	0	22	62	196	25	66	1	1	.303	.454	.756	.2
Playoffs	12	45	6	13	3	0	4	11	28	2	6	0	1	.327	.622	.949	.28
Career	504	1,722	220	439	89	3	74	251	756	102	276	4	6	.303	.439	.743	.2

Was as good as anyone at third base defensively, and while his average was again disappointing, no one had more clutch hits in September and October. In the end, he emerged from his shy shell to become one of the leaders.

PABLO OZUNA

Second base
Bats: Right **Throws:** Right
Height: 5-10 **Weight:** 185
Age: 31 **ML Exp.:** 4 yrs.

	G	AB	R	H	2B	3B	HR	RBI	TB	BB	SO	SB	CS	OBP	SLG	OPS	AV
Season	70	203	27	56	7	2	0	11	67	7	26	14	7	.313	.330	.643	.2
Playoffs	2	0	1	0	0	0	0	0	0	0	0	1	0	.000	.000	.000	.0
Career	135	314	38	85	11	4	0	16	104	10	37	19	8	.307	.331	.638	.2

The most valuable off the bench, he came as a non-roster invitee to spring training. Made 52 starts at five positions and hit .276 while doing it. Finished fourth on the team with 14 stolen bases.

TIMO PEREZ

Left field
Bats: Left **Throws:** Left
Height: 5-9 **Weight:** 180
Age: 30 **ML Exp.:** 6 yrs.

	G	AB	R	H	2B	3B	HR	RBI	TB	BB	SO	SB	CS	OBP	SLG	OPS	AV
Season	76	179	13	39	8	0	2	15	53	12	25	2	2	.266	.296	.562	.2
Playoffs	2	2	0	0	0	0	0	0	0	0	0	0	0	.000	.000	.000	.0
Career	551	1,550	172	408	81	8	25	169	580	83	149	22	22	.302	.374	.676	.2

A valuable extra outfielder and left-handed bat off the bench, Perez also made 39 starts while displaying a strong arm in the outfield.

CHRIS WIDGER

Catcher
Bats: Right Throws: Right
Height: 6-2 Weight: 215
Age: 34 ML Exp.: 9 yrs.

	G	AB	R	H	2B	3B	HR	RBI	TB	BB	SO	SB	CS	OBP	SLG	OPS	AVG
Season	45	141	18	34	8	0	4	11	54	10	22	0	2	.296	.383	.679	.241
Playoffs	1	1	0	0	0	0	0	1	0	2	1	0	0	.667	0	0	.667
Career	577	1,733	174	419	101	7	54	213	696	130	360	10	9	.299	.402	.700	.242

Picked up from the Independent League, Widger was popular and productive. In his first major-league season since 2003, Widger hit four homers, drove in 11 and was nearly flawless as a catcher.

WILLIE HARRIS

Second base
Bats: Left Throws: Right
Height: 5-9 Weight: 170
Age: 27 ML Exp.: 5 yrs.

	G	AB	R	H	2B	3B	HR	RBI	TB	BB	SO	SB	CS	OBP	SLG	OPS	AVG
Season	56	121	17	31	2	1	1	8	38	13	25	10	3	.333	.314	.647	.256
Playoffs	3	2	1	2	0	0	0	1	2	0	0	1	0	1.000	1.000	2.000	1.000
Career	322	854	121	207	25	4	5	52	255	83	160	49	12	.309	.299	.608	.242

Lost his starting second-base job and spent time in the minors, but Harris came back to go 11 for 29 (.379) in his final 16 games. He made 32 appearances at second and five at shortstop.

FRANK THOMAS

Designated hitter
Bats: Right Throws: Right
Height: 6-5 Weight: 275
Age: 37 ML Exp.: 16 yrs.

	G	AB	R	H	2B	3B	HR	RBI	TB	BB	SO	SB	CS	OBP	SLG	OPS	AVG
Season	34	105	19	23	3	0	12	26	62	16	31	0	0	.315	.590	.905	.219
Playoffs	—	—	—	—	—	—	—	—	—	—	—	—	—	—	—	—	—
Career	1,959	6,956	1,327	2,136	447	11	448	1,456	3,949	1,466	1,165	32	23	.427	.568	.995	.307

Best hitter in franchise history was limited to 34 games due to injury. Still, produced 12 homers and 26 RBIs and provided needed midseason boost.

GEOFF BLUM

Third base
Bats: Switch Throws: Right
Height: 6-3 Weight: 200
Age: 32 ML Exp.: 7 yrs.

	G	AB	R	H	2B	3B	HR	RBI	TB	BB	SO	SB	CS	OBP	SLG	OPS	AVG
Season	31	95	6	19	2	1	1	3	26	4	15	0	1	.232	.274	.696	.200
Playoffs	2	2	1	1	0	0	1	1	4	0	0	0	0	1.000	4.000	5.000	1.000
Career	791	2,375	284	596	127	10	62	277	929	207	400	18	15	.314	.391	.705	.251

Added at the trading deadline, the versatile and popular Blum had his most notable moment when he hit the game-winning homer in the 14th inning of Game 3 of the World Series. Played all four infield spots in 24 starts.

BRANDON MCCARTHY

Pitcher | Bats: Right | Throws: Right | Height: 6-7 | Weight: 190 | Age: 22 | ML Exp.: 1 yr.

	G	GS	CG	IP	H	R	ER	HR	BB	SO	W	L	ERA
Season	12	10	0	67	62	30	30	13	17	48	3	2	4.03
Career	12	10	0	67	62	30	30	13	17	48	3	2	4.03

SHINGO TAKATSU

Pitcher | Bats: Right | Throws: Right | Height: 6-0 | Weight: 180 | Age: 35 | ML Exp.: 2 yrs.

	G	GS	CG	IP	H	R	ER	HR	BB	SO	W	L	ERA
Season	31	0	0	28.7	41	21	21	11	19	38	2	2	5.97
Career	99	0	0	98.2	81	38	37	17	40	88	8	6	3.38

JON ADKINS

Pitcher | Bats: Left | Throws: Right | Height: 5-11 | Weight: 215 | Age: 28 | ML Exp.: 3 yrs.

	G	GS	CG	IP	H	R	ER	HR	BB	SO	W	L	ERA
Season	5	0	0	8.1	13	8	8	0	4	1	0	4	8.64
Career	59	0	0	79.2	96	48	45	14	31	48	2	1	5.08

KEVIN WALKER

Pitcher | Bats: Left | Throws: Left | Height: 6-3 | Weight: 215 | Age: 29 | ML Exp.: 6 yrs.

	G	GS	CG	IP	H	R	ER	HR	BB	SO	W	L	ERA
Season	9	0	0	7	10	7	7	1	5	5	0	1	9.00
Career	122	0	0	102	84	59	54	10	63	95	7	3	4.76

JEFF BAJENARU

Pitcher | Bats: Right | Throws: Right | Height: 6-1 | Weight: 200 | Age: 27 | ML Exp.: 2 yrs.

	G	GS	CG	IP	H	R	ER	HR	BB	SO	W	L	ERA
Season	4	0	0	4.1	4	3	3	2	0	3	0	0	6.23
Career	13	0	0	12.2	19	13	13	2	6	11	0	1	9.24

DAVID SANDERS

Pitcher | Bats: Left | Throws: Left | Height: 6-0 | Weight: 200 | Age: 26 | ML Exp.: 2 yrs.

	G	GS	CG	IP	H	R	ER	HR	BB	SO	W	L	ERA
Season	2	0	0	2	3	3	3	1	1	1	0	0	13.50
Career	22	0	0	24	28	19	18	6	12	15	0	0	6.75

ROSS GLOAD

17 | First base | Bats: Left | Throws: Left | Height: 6-0 | Weight: 200 | Age: 29 | ML Exp.: 4 yrs.

	G	AB	R	H	2B	3B	TB	BB	SO	SB	HR	RBI	AVG
Season	28	42	2	7	2	0	9	2	9	0	0	5	.167
Career	182	338	38	96	19	1	144	28	63	0	3	56	.284

BRIAN ANDERSON

44 | Right field | Bats: Right | Throws: Right | Height: 6-2 | Weight: 205 | Age: 23 | ML Exp.: 1 yr.

	G	AB	R	H	2B	3B	TB	BB	SO	SB	HR	RBI	AVG
Season	13	34	3	6	1	0	13	0	12	1	2	3	.176
Career	13	34	3	6	1	0	13	0	12	1	2	3	.176

JOE BORCHARD

25 | Center field | Bats: Switch | Throws: Right | Height: 6-5 | Weight: 220 | Age: 26 | ML Exp.: 4 yrs.

	G	AB	R	H	2B	3B	TB	BB	SO	SB	HR	RBI	AVG
Season	7	12	0	5	2	0	7	0	4	0	0	0	.417
Career	102	298	36	57	7	1	102	25	93	1	12	30	.191

PEDRO LOPEZ

62 | Second base | Bats: Right | Throws: Right | Height: 6-1 | Weight: 160 | Age: 21 | ML Exp.: 1 yr.

	G	AB	R	H	2B	3B	TB	BB	SO	SB	HR	RBI	AVG
Season	2	7	1	2	0	0	2	0	1	0	0	2	.286
Career	2	7	1	2	0	0	2	0	1	0	0	2	.286

RAUL CASANOVA

31 | Catcher | Bats: Switch | Throws: Right | Height: 6-0 | Weight: 230 | Age: 33 | ML Exp.: 7 yrs.

	G	AB	R	H	2B	3B	TB	BB	SO	SB	HR	RBI	AVG
Season	6	5	0	1	0	0	1	0	1	0	0	0	.200
Career	338	947	81	220	37	4	349	85	173	2	28	113	.232

JAMIE BURKE

27 | Catcher | Bats: Right | Throws: Right | Height: 6-0 | Weight: 225 | Age: 34 | ML Exp.: 3 yrs.

	G	AB	R	H	2B	3B	TB	BB	SO	SB	HR	RBI	AVG
Season	1	1	0	0	0	0	0	0	0	0	0	0	.000
Career	73	134	23	44	9	0	53	10	15	0	0	17	.328

DATE	OPPONENT	SCORE	PITCHER OF RECORD	REC.	QUICK HIT
April 4	Cleveland	W 1-0	Mark Buehrle	1-0	Buehrle (8 IP, 2 H, 103 NP) retired 1st 12 in 1:51 game; Rowand drove in Konerko for lone run
April 6	Cleveland	W 4-3	Damaso Marte	2-0	Konerko, Dye back-to-back HRs drove 4-run 9th inning; Garcia (2 R, 5 H, 6 IP, 3 BB) struck out six
April 7	Cleveland	L 11-5 (11)	Luis Vizcaino	2-1	Tribe exacted late-inning revenge, scoring six in 11th; Contreras (ER, 4 H) pitches 6 IP, gets ND
April 8	@ Minnesota	W 5-1	Orlando Hernandez	3-1	Hernandez (1 ER, 5 K) threw 70 of 104 pitches for strikes over 7 IP; Konerko, Rowand homered
April 9	@ Minnesota	W 8-5	Jon Garland	4-1	Everett, Perez, Konerko homered to support Garland, who allowed 3 ER on 10 hits over 6 innings
April 10	@ Minnesota	L 5-2	Mark Buehrle	4-2	Hunter HR broke Buehrle (7 IP, 5 ER, 7 H) streak of 17 straight scoreless IP; Sox left 8 on base
April 11	@ Cleveland	W 2-1	Freddy Garcia	5-2	Garcia (8 IP, 4 H, ER, 2 BB, 4 K) aided by RBI singles by Everett and Podsednik
April 13	@ Cleveland	W 5-4 (10)	Luis Vizcaino	6-2	Contreras (5 H, 4 ER) walked 5 in 6⅔ IP; Uribe sacrifice fly in 10th inning toppled Indians
April 14	@ Cleveland	L 8-6	Orlando Hernandez	6-3	Hernandez (5 IP, 6 R) 4-1 with 2.25 ERA in 7 April starts since '02; Everett injured left shoulder
April 15	Seattle	W 6-4	Jon Garland	7-3	Garland took perfect game into 7th, retiring 1st 19; Sox hung on behind 4 relievers in 9th inning
April 16	Seattle	W 2-1	Mark Buehrle	8-3	In 1 hr., 39 min; Buehrle pitched CG 3-hitter, striking out career-high 12; Konerko homered twice
April 17	Seattle	L 5-4	Freddy Garcia	8-4	Crede's 9th-inn. single (8-gm. hit streak) closed gap to 5-4; Harris' failed 2nd base steal final out
April 18	Minnesota	W 5-4	Luis Vizcaino	9-4	Everett put Sox in sole possession of 1st by smacking 2 HRs; Rusty Takatsu allowed homer
April 19	Minnesota	W 3-1	Orlando Hernandez	10-4	Sox completed 2-game sweep of defending AL Central champs despite allowing 14 hits
April 20	@ Detroit	W 9-1	Jon Garland	11-4	Garland improved to 3-0 (8 innings, 5 hits) and Dye snapped 0-for-11 slump with 2-run HR and 4 RBIs
April 21	@ Detroit	W 4-3	Mark Buehrle	12-4	Podsednik bailed out Buehrle with 2-run single in 7th that gave Sox lead; Takatsu pitched 9th
April 22	@ Kansas City	W 8-2	Freddy Garcia	13-4	Wins equal franchise's best start (1912, 1919, 1935); Crede ran career-high hit streak to 13 (3 hits)
April 23	@ Kansas City	W 3-2 (10)	Damaso Marte	14-4	Rowand came off bench to hit game-winning single with 2 outs; Contreras left in 4th (hamstring)
April 24	@ Kansas City	W 4-3	Neal Cotts	15-4	Won despite 4 errors and Hernandez walking 6 batters in 5 innings; 3rd straight series sweep
April 25	@ Oakland	W 6-0	Jon Garland	16-4	Garland scattered 4 hits and walked just one in pitching 3rd CG of career, hasn't allowed HR in 25 inn.
April 26	@ Oakland	L 9-7	Damaso Marte	16-5	Sox tagged Harden for 6 runs in 5 innings, but blew pair of three-run leads; Ozuna needed X-rays (HBP)
April 27	@ Oakland	L 2-1	Damaso Marte	16-6	Guillen, Crede tossed for arguing calls; depleted lineup (Uribe, Iguchi, Ozuna out) went 6-2 on road trip
April 29	Detroit	L 3-2 (11)	Shingo Takatsu	16-7	1st time losing opening gm. of series; reason: 16 runners stranded (runner on every inn. but 11th)
April 30	Detroit	W 4-3	Orlando Hernandez	17-7	Sox 10-3 in 1-run games and have led every game (24); Hernandez squeaked by (118 pitches)
May 1	Detroit	W 8-0	Jon Garland	18-7	Garland threw 2nd straight 4-hit shutout by inducing 11 groundouts; Everett (3 RBIs) hitting star
May 3	Kansas City	W 5-4	Mark Buehrle	19-7	Buehrle gave up 3 HRs but bats heated up in 8th behind Iguchi's 4th hit and Everett's 2-run double
May 4	Kansas City	W 4-2	Freddy Garcia	20-7	Fifth straight win over Kansas City; Garcia has pitched at least 6 innings in each of 6 starts
May 5	Kansas City	W 2-1	Jose Contreras	21-7	Two runs in 8th without a hit—4 walks, hit batsman—Podsednik drew bases-loaded walk to score Dye
May 6	@ Toronto	W 5-3	Orlando Hernandez	22-7	Konerko snapped 0-for-23 slump with single in 8th and Pierzynski's two-run single broke 3-3 tie
May 7	@ Toronto	W 10-7	Jon Garland	23-7	Garland was given 10-2 lead after 4 inn.; Cotts pitched 2 perfect innings in second app. since April 24
May 8	@ Toronto	W 5-4	Mark Buehrle	24-7	Sox posted second 8-game winning streak but nearly blew 5-0 lead after committing 2 errors
May 9	@ Tampa Bay	L 4-2	Freddy Garcia	24-8	Ex-Sox Singleton had 2 RBI singles off Garcia; Sox failed to score after 4th inn. for 3rd straight game
May 10	@ Tampa Bay	L 7-6	Shingo Takatsu	24-9	Takatsu gave up HR to Jorge Cantu in 9th; Guillen bemoaned 9 walks by Contreras, Vizcaino, Marte
May 11	@ Tampa Bay	W 5-2	Orlando Hernandez	25-9	Avoided three-game sweep thanks to Hernandez and Hermanson (only AL reliever not to allow run)
May 12	Baltimore	W 3-2	Jon Garland	26-9	Garland AL's first 7-game winner (won last 9 starts) but allowed 1st HR at home (Rafael Palmeiro in 5th)
May 13	Baltimore	W 5-3	Mark Buehrle	27-9	Three-run rally in 7th behind infield hit, 2 walks, error and Konerko's run, broken-bat single
May 14	Baltimore	L 9-6	Freddy Garcia	27-10	Podsednik stole 4 bases (37) and beat out 10th, 11th infield hits; Garcia allowed season-high 7 runs
May 15	Baltimore	L 6-2	Jose Contreras	27-11	Streak of 37 straight games with lead ended (tied for 3rd longest); Contreras left after 7th (2 HRs)
May 16	Texas	L 7-6	Damaso Marte	27-12	Kevin Mench hit 2nd of 2 HRs in 9th; Hernandez lasted only 2⅔ innings (shortest for Sox starter)
May 17	Texas	W 5-2	Jon Garland	28-12	Garland's eighth win prevented season-high, 4-game losing streak; Hermanson earned 9th save (0 ER)
May 18	Texas	W 7-0	Mark Buehrle	29-12	No. 4 batter Konerko (3 hits, HR) and No. 6 batter Dye (3 doubles) supported Buehrle (7 inn., 0 ER, 9 hits)
May 20	@ Cubs	W 5-1	Freddy Garcia	30-12	Cubs starter Maddux plunked Iguchi, Sox starter Garcia (5 hits) hit Jerry Hairston, Derrek Lee in 1st
May 21	@ Cubs	W 5-3	Jose Contreras	31-12	Zambrano strong (1 hit, 7 inn.), but bullpen not: 2-out, 2-run, single (Konerko), 2-run double (Everett)
May 22	@ Cubs	L 4-3	Luis Vizcaino	31-13	Rookie McCarthy made MLB debut (left with 2-1 lead, 78 pitches), but Vizcaino give up 3-run HR
May 23	@ L.A. Angels	L 4-0	Jon Garland	31-14	Garland lost 1st game, Sox blanked for 1st time; Santana, making 2nd career start, gave up just 5 hits
May 24	@ L.A. Angels	W 2-1 (11)	Damaso Marte	32-14	Managed only 5 hits, but Iguchi ripped 2-out double in 11th, scoring Crede; 4th win in 18 tries at LA
May 25	@ L.A. Angels	W 4-2	Freddy Garcia	33-14	Garcia raised lifetime record vs. Angels to 11-3, has allowed just two ER in 15 innings in last 2 starts
May 26	@ L.A. Angels	L 3-2	Jose Contreras	33-15	Contreras' solid start (9 K, 2 hits in 1st 6 inn.) ruined in 7th with 2-out, 2-run HR by Dallas McPherson
May 27	Texas	L 6-2	Brandon McCarthy	33-16	McCarthy yielded 4 HRs and lost 2nd straight (back to minors); Rangers have 21 HRs in 7 games
May 28	Texas				Game postponed by rain; rescheduled as Aug. 30 double-header
May 29	Texas	L 12-4	Jon Garland	33-17	Sox finished road trip vs. Cubs, Angels and Rangers with 4-5 record; Rangers pounded out 3 more HRs
May 30	L.A. Angels	W 5-4	Cliff Politte	34-17	Thomas played for 1st time (2 AB, BB, run) but left in 7th (strained hip flexor); 14th comeback win
May 31	L.A. Angels	W 5-4	Cliff Politte	35-17	Marte blew 2nd straight save chance, Politte pitched perfect 9th; Dye lined HR off Donnelly in 9th
June 1	L.A. Angels	L 10-7	Kevin Walker	35-18	Perez (error), Walker (4 runs in 7th), Vizcaino (2-run single) and Hermanson (2 runs in 9th) unravel
June 3	Cleveland	W 6-4	Orlando Hernandez	36-18	19-4 vs. Central; Everett, Dye had 2 RBIs, Cotts (1 hitless inn.) and Hermanson (12th save)
June 4	Cleveland	W 6-5	Jon Garland	37-18	Hermanson nearly blew 2-run lead after 2 fluke hits trimmed lead; win guaranteed 14th series win in 18
June 5	Cleveland	L 6-4 (12)	Dustin Hermanson	37-19	Hermanson walked 2 in 12th, wild pitch to 3rd scored run; scored on in 3 of last 4 appearances
June 6	@ Colorado	W 9-3	Freddy Garcia	38-19	Garcia allowed 3-run shot to Brad Hawpe in 1st but then retired next 22 batters; Sox cranked out 15 hits
June 7	@ Colorado	W 2-1	Jose Contreras	39-19	4th-inn. rally started with Konerko's double (1,000th career hit); Cotts/Hermanson throw 3 perfect inn.
June 8	@ Colorado	W 15-5	Orlando Hernandez	40-19	Season highs: 15 runs, 22 hits, 6-run inn.; score 10 in final two inn., including Thomas' pinch-hit HR
June 10	@ San Diego	W 4-2	Jon Garland	41-19	Garland didn't yield hit until 5th and was scoreless through 6th; win made him AL's 1st 10-game winner
June 11	@ San Diego	L 2-1	Dustin Hermanson	41-20	Hermanson tagged for 2 runs with 2 outs in 9th, ending 15 straight save streak; Buehrle gem wasted
June 12	@ San Diego	W 8-5 (10)	Cliff Politte	42-20	Rowand's 3-run HR in 10th off Hoffman sent Sox home happy, awaiting 2-week, 12-game homestand
June 13	Arizona	L 8-1	Jose Contreras	42-21	D'backs scored 6 times on 6 consecutive hits in the 2nd inn. off Contreras, who yielded 8 runs in start
June 14	Arizona	L 10-4	Orlando Hernandez	42-22	Hernandez (2 HRs, 6 runs) has allowed 4 ERs or more in 4 straight; Konerko's hit streak at 11
June 15	Arizona	W 12-6	Jon Garland	43-22	Season-high 10 runs in the 6th highlighted by 3 HRs (solo by Thomas, 3-run shots by Konerko, Uribe)
June 17	L.A. Dodgers	W 6-0	Mark Buehrle	44-22	Buehrle notched 1st shutout behind offense by Konerko (13-gm. hit streak) and HRs by Dye, Thomas

	OPPONENT		SCORE	PITCHER OF RECORD	REC.	QUICK HIT
June 18		L.A. Dodgers	W 5-3	Cliff Politte	45-22	Stymied by 3 H, unearned run in 1st 8 inn., Sox score 4 runs in 9th led by Pierzynski's 2-out, 2-run HR
June 19		L.A. Dodgers	W 4-3	Cliff Politte	46-22	Rowand put Sox ahead in 8th with 2-run single; Politte earned 2nd win and Hermanson got 16th save
June 20		Kansas City	W 11-8	Neal Cotts	47-22	17-hit attack bailed out McCarthy and reliever Vizcaino; Thomas increased HR total to 6 in just 32 AB
June 21		Kansas City	W 5-1	Jon Garland	48-22	Garland (4 H, 8⅓ inn.) earned 12th win, now 5-0 vs. Central; no extra-base ended for 1st time in 43 gms
June 22		Kansas City	W 5-1	Mark Buehrle	49-22	Everett's 3-run HR provided cushion for Buehrle, whose career-high streak of 25 scoreless inn. ended
June 24		Cubs	W 12-2	Freddy Garcia	50-22	All-around game featured 3 HRs, 3 stolen bases; largest margin of victory in 46-game series vs. Cubs
June 25		Cubs	L 6-2	Jose Contreras	50-23	Contreras (3-4) gave up 1st-inning grand slam to Aramis Ramirez for 2nd rough outing in 3 starts
June 26		Cubs	L 2-0	Jon Garland	50-24	Prior (6 inn., 1 hit) outdueled Garland (retired 1st 10 batters) in 1st start since fracturing elbow bone
June 28		@ Detroit	W 2-1	Mark Buehrle	51-24	Hermanson completed his biggest escape after allowing leadoff triple to Ivan Rodriguez, retired next 3
June 29		@ Detroit	W 4-3 (13)	Shingo Takatsu	52-24	Thomas snapped 0-for-13 slump with HR in 13th (8 HRs, 52 AB); Takatsu (2⅔ inn.) earned 1st win
June 30		@ Detroit	W 6-1	Freddy Garcia	53-24	Improved to 26-5 vs. Central, 18-7 mark in June; Crede's 3-run blast in 5th erased 1-0 Sox deficit
July 1		@ Oakland	L 6-2	Jose Contreras	53-25	3 pitchers messy with 4 walks, wild pitch; Contreras' 30-pitch 4th inn. allowed A's to erase 2-run hole
July 2		@ Oakland	W 5-3	Jon Garland	54-25	Sox snapped 3-game losing skid vs. A's; Garland became MLB's 1st 13-game winner
July 3		@ Oakland	L 7-2	Mark Buehrle	54-26	Buehrle surrendered career-high 14 hits, including 6 during 4-run 6th, to snap his 9-gm. win streak
July 4		Tampa Bay	W 10-8	Luis Vizcaino	55-26	Dye notched career-tying 6 RBIs, but McCarthy demoted after yielding 5 runs in 3 innings (8.14 ERA)
July 5		Tampa Bay	W 6-4	Cliff Politte	56-26	DH Thomas launched 3-run HR in 8th (17 hits, 10 HRs this season); Dye also homered (19 total)
July 6		Tampa Bay	W 7-2	Jose Contreras	57-26	Podsednik named to All-Star team during game, Thomas continued surge with 3-run shot in 5th
July 8		Oakland	L 4-2	Jon Garland	57-27	Garland had shortest outing (5 inn., 8 hits) since Aug. 19 and fell to 0-2 in last 2 home starts
July 9		Oakland	L 10-1	Mark Buehrle	57-28	Buehrle lost to Zito for 2nd straight outing; defeat 1st time Garland and Buehrle lost in succession
July 10		Oakland	L 9-8 (11)	Luis Vizcaino	57-29	Sox wasted 5-hit game by Konerko; head into break with 9-gm. lead over Twins, league-best 3.62 ERA
July 14		@ Cleveland	W 1-0	Jose Contreras	58-29	Lone run came in 1st with Thomas' double that scored Iguchi; Contreras hurled 7 shutout innings
July 15		@ Cleveland	W 7-1	Freddy Garcia	59-29	Ozuna recorded 1st 4-hit game (started for resting Crede), Sox scored 4 in 1st to give Garcia cushion
July 16		@ Cleveland	W 7-5	Mark Buehrle	60-29	Jumped to 6-0 lead starting with 2-out rally in 2nd; Buehrle hit Hafner in face (1st HBP this season)
July 17		@ Cleveland	W 4-0	Jon Garland	61-29	1st 4-gm. sweep in Cleveland in 42 yrs. extended AL Central lead to season-high 12 games
July 18		Detroit	W 7-5	Luis Vizcaino	62-29	Erupted for 5 runs on 3 HRs off Douglass in 7th; Magglio Ordonez returned (2 for 3, walk)
July 19		Detroit	L 7-1	Jose Contreras	62-30	All runs on Contreras (12 straight retired before 6th) came with 2 outs; 11-game streak vs. Central gone
July 20		Detroit	L 8-6	Freddy Garcia	62-31	Garcia entered game 13-1 in last 18 day games, but charged with 6 runs in 4th loss in 13 decisions
July 21		Boston	L 6-5	Luis Vizcaino	62-32	Crede's dropped foul pop with one out in 9th costly as Manny Ramirez hit HR on next pitch for win
July 22		Boston	W 8-4	Jon Garland	63-32	Pierzynski and Uribe each hit 3-run homers in 6th; Wakefield limited Sox to 3 hits through 1st 5 innings
July 23		Boston	L 3-0	Orlando Hernandez	63-33	Third shutout of season; stranded 5 runners in scoring position; Hernandez (4 hits, 6⅔) strong
July 24		Boston	L 6-4	Jose Contreras	64-33	Sox scored 4 of 6 runs with 2 outs to split series with defending world champs; 3-4 on homestand
July 25		@ Kansas City	W 14-6	Freddy Garcia	65-33	Dye returned after missing 4 games (staph infection in leg) and Sox pounded 22 hits to support Garcia
July 26		@ Kansas City	L 7-1	Mark Buehrle	65-34	Buehrle extended streak of lasting at least 6 inn. to 49, but tagged for 6 runs in 6th; Sox commit 3 E
July 27		@ Kansas City	L 6-5 (13)	Luis Vizcaino	65-35	Gload's error on potential double-play grounder preceded Mike Sweeney's 3-run, gm.-tying HR in 8th
July 29		@ Baltimore	W 7-2	Orlando Hernandez	66-35	Hernandez limited O's to 2 runs over 6 inn., pitched at least 6 innings for 3rd time since coming off DL
July 30		@ Baltimore	W 9-6	Neal Cotts	67-35	Pierzynski smacked 3-run HR in 8th to erase 6-4 hole; Iguchi (2-4) 10-for-20 with 6 RBIs in last 5 games
July 31		@ Baltimore	W 9-4	Freddy Garcia	68-35	Scored 8 runs in 1st 2 inn.; Iguchi (bruised hip) left game after reliever Todd Williams hit him in 3rd
Aug. 1		@ Baltimore	W 6-3	Mark Buehrle	69-35	Buehrle tossed in 6th for throwing at batter (streak of 6 inn. pitched snapped); 15-game lead in Central
Aug. 2		Toronto	L 7-3	Jon Garland	69-36	Garland allowed 13 hits (career high); Guillen tossed (2nd of season) for arguing strike zone in 4th
Aug. 3		Toronto	L 4-3	Orlando Hernandez	69-37	Sox fell to 3-9 in last 12 home games; stranded 6 runners in scoring position; Everett, Konerko homer
Aug. 4		Toronto	W 5-4	Luis Vizcaino	70-37	Iguchi poked opposite-field HR off reliever Speier in the 8th; Hermanson struck out the side in the 9th
Aug. 5		Seattle	L 4-2	Freddy Garcia	70-38	Small ball gone? Rowand and Pierzynski each HR (in last 3 games, 9 of 10 runs scored on home runs)
Aug. 6		Seattle	W 4-2	Mark Buehrle	71-38	Buehrle made quick work (2 hrs. 19 min.), allowing 1 run in 7 innings; Konerko hit 2-run HR in 1st
Aug. 7		Seattle	W 3-1	Jon Garland	72-38	Rowand saved game in 8th with wall-banging catch off Richie Sexson's bat; Garland (16-5) left in 8th
Aug. 8		@ N.Y. Yankees	L 3-2	Orlando Hernandez	72-39	Hernandez's (3 runs, 4 hits, 6 innings) homecoming spoiled by 2-run HR by Alex Rodriguez in 1st
Aug. 9		@ N.Y. Yankees	W 2-1	Jose Contreras	73-39	Konerko, Iguchi homered to support Contreras (7-plus scoreless innings); Sox 34 games over .500
Aug. 10		@ N.Y. Yankees	W 2-1 (10)	Neal Cotts	74-39	Scored off closer Rivera (1st time since June 24, 2000) with Podsednik's bunt to bring in Uribe
Aug. 12		@ Boston	L 9-8	Mark Buehrle	74-40	Buehrle peppered for 12 hits (every Red Sox starter had at least 1), including David Ortiz's 2 homers
Aug. 13		@ Boston	L 7-4	Jon Garland	74-41	3 of the 4 runs came on solo home runs, Ozuna and Iguchi went combined 0-for-8 at the top of order
Aug. 14		@ Boston				Game postponed (by rain); rescheduled Sept. 5
Aug. 15		Minnesota	L 4-2	Jose Contreras	74-42	Contreras had tough 4th (4 runs, 2 walks that set up 2-run singles); Podsednik on 15-day DL (groin)
Aug. 16		Minnesota	L 9-4 (16)	Jon Adkins	74-43	Hermanson surrendered game-tying HR in 9th, Adkins allowed 5 runs in 16th (5 hrs, 9 min. game)
Aug. 17		Minnesota	L 5-1	Mark Buehrle	74-44	Sweep means losing baseball's best record (Cardinals 76-44); Everett's single in 7th broke up no-hitter
Aug. 19		N.Y. Yankees	L 3-1	Jon Garland	74-45	Garland gave up 7 singles (5 in the 3rd, 5th when NY scored); haven't won since Podsednik put on DL
Aug. 20		N.Y. Yankees	L 5-0	Orlando Hernandez	74-46	Sox scored just 2 runs in last 36 innings; Iguchi had 2 of team's 4 hits, but Sox were 0-11 with RSP
Aug. 21		N.Y. Yankees	W 6-2	Jose Contreras	75-46	Erupted for 4 HRs in 6-run 4th inning off Randy Johnson; 8½-game lead
Aug. 23		@ Minnesota	L 1-0	Freddy Garcia	75-47	Jacque Jones' HR cost Garcia a no-hitter and shutout in 8th; Ozuna had 2 of team's 3 hits
Aug. 24		@ Minnesota	W 6-4	Mark Buehrle	76-47	Offense broke out of rut with 13 hits to support Buehrle; Hermanson back for 1st time since Aug. 16
Aug. 25		@ Minnesota	W 2-1 (10)	Dustin Hermanson	77-47	Jenks earned first MLB save; Blum led off 10th with double and scored from 3rd on Perez's single
Aug. 26		@ Seattle	W 5-3 (12)	Luis Vizcaino	78-47	Sox squeezed out win behind Anderson's 1st 2 career HRs along with Iguchi's 13th homer of season
Aug. 27		@ Seattle	W 4-3	Jose Contreras	79-47	Pierzynski's sweeping tag on Ichiro Suzuki prevented Seattle from tying game in 8th
Aug. 28		@ Seattle	L 9-2	Freddy Garcia	79-48	Garcia pounded for 11 hits in shortest outing of season (season-high 8 runs, 4⅓ innings)
Aug. 29		@ Texas	L 7-5	Mark Buehrle	79-49	Iguchi committed season-high 3 errors, including 2 during 3-run 4th; Buehrle lost 1st gm. vs. Texas
Aug. 30		@ Texas	L 8-6	Jon Garland	79-50	Garland lost 3rd straight, is 1-3 with 4.78 ERA in August; Rowand went 3 for 4 with double, 3 RBIs
Aug. 30		@ Texas	W 8-0	Brandon McCarthy	80-50	McCarthy (2 hits, 7⅔ innings) didn't allow hit until 5th, gave Sox split of twi-night doubleheader
Aug. 31		@ Texas	L 9-2	Orlando Hernandez	80-51	August done: 12-16 record (1st losing month since Aug. '04); Uribe, Harris produced 4 of team's 6 hits
Sept. 1		Detroit	W 12-3	Jose Contreras	81-51	Pierzynski 3-for-3 with 3 RBIs; team had season-high 9 extra-base hits and scored 10 runs for 8th time

	OPPONENT		SCORE		PITCHER OF RECORD	REC.	QUICK HIT
Sept. 2		Detroit	W	9-1	Freddy Garcia	82-51	Sox registered 9 hits for 10th win in 13 tries vs. Detroit; big guns Everett, Uribe each hit 3-run home runs
Sept. 3	D	Detroit	W	6-2	Mark Buehrle	83-51	Rowand, Dye hit back-to-back HRs in 7th inning; Iguchi returned (HR shy of cycle)
Sept. 4		Detroit	W	2-0	Jon Garland	84-51	Garland (4 hits, 7 strikeouts) earned 1st win since Aug. 7; 3-0 with 0.35 ERA vs. Detroit this season
Sept. 5	B	@ Boston	W	5-3	Brandon McCarthy	85-51	McCarthy scattered 3 hits, struck out career-high 7 in 7 innings; final 2 runs on HRs by Konerko, Uribe
Sept. 6		Kansas City	W	6-5	Orlando Hernandez	86-51	Marte gave up 2-run HR in 8th, but Politte, Hermanson combine for final 5 outs; Royals 0-7 at the Cell
Sept. 7	KC	Kansas City	W	1-0	Jose Contreras	87-51	Contreras walked 5 but earned 4th straight win; Marte hit 2 in 9th, but Hermanson closed it out
Sept. 8		Kansas City	L	4-2	Freddy Garcia	87-52	Managed just 2 hits vs. rookie Howell, 3 relievers; Garcia hung slider to Angel Berroa for 2-run HR
Sept. 9		L.A. Angels	L	6-5 (12)	Dustin Hermanson	87-53	V. Guerrero doubled off Hermanson and scored from 2nd on sac bunt in 12th; Konerko: 2 doubles, HR
Sept. 10	A	L.A. Angels	L	10-5	Jon Garland	87-54	Garland lost for 2nd time in 3 starts after allowing 3-run HR in 5th; Central lead down to 6 1/2
Sept. 11		L.A. Angels	L	6-1	Orlando Hernandez	87-55	Hernandez knocked out after 2 innings (3 1st-inning homers); offense faltered: 0 for 9 with RSP
Sept. 13		@ Kansas City	W	6-4	Jose Contreras	88-55	Survived 2 rain delays, Contreras limited KC to 2 hits through 5 innings; Jenks pitched scoreless 8th, 9th
Sept. 14	KC	@ Kansas City	L	10-9	Dustin Hermanson	88-56	Hermanson's 4th blown save in 38 chances; Sox homered 3 times, but committed 3 fielding errors
Sept. 15		@ Kansas City	L	7-5	Mark Buehrle	88-57	Buehrle (6 1/3 IP, 4 R, 9 H) 12-6 career vs. Royals; after losing 10, Kansas City won 5 of 8 against Sox
Sept. 16		@ Minnesota	W	2-1 (10)	Bobby Jenks	89-57	3 singles, sac bunt in 10th gave Sox 4 1/2-game lead; Jenks pitched scorless 1 1/3 innings for 1st win
Sept. 17	C	@ Minnesota	L	5-0	Orlando Hernandez	89-58	Santana struck out 13 in 8 shutout inn.; Hernandez (9.00 ERA last 4 starts) yanked after 3 2/3 innings
Sept. 18		@ Minnesota	W	2-1	Jose Contreras	90-58	Mere 3 1/2-game lead entering series with Indians; Contreras (5 hits over 8 innings) won again
Sept. 19		Cleveland	L	7-5	Damaso Marte	90-59	Everett homered to break tie in 7th, but Aaron's Boone's 2-run, 2-out single in 8th took lead away
Sept. 20	C	Cleveland	W	7-6 (10)	Dustin Hermanson	91-59	Crede 2 HR, including game-winner; Sox 56-32 in games decided by 2 R or less; Buehrle gave up 3 HR
Sept. 21		Cleveland	L	8-0	Jon Garland	91-60	Indians' Travis Hafner had 2 HR, 5 RBIs; Scott Elarton threw 7 1/3 shutout innings
Sept. 22		Minnesota	L	4-1 (11)	Bobby Jenks	91-61	Sox left 8 on base, turned 4 DP; McCarthy (8 IP, 4 K, ER) matched Santana, who is 0.92 vs. Sox in '05
Sept. 23	C	Minnesota	W	3-1	Jose Contreras	92-61	Dye lined 3-run homer over left-field wall in 1st; Contreras pitched 1st career CG (6 H, 1 BB, 9 K)
Sept. 24		Minnesota	W	8-1	Freddy Garcia	93-61	Dye (3-run), Crede (solo) hit HRs in 6-run 3rd off nemesis Joe Mays; Garcia strong over 8 IP (4 H, 1 ER)
Sept. 25		Minnesota	W	4-1	Mark Buehrle	94-61	Buehrle (6 K, 0 BB) tossed 4-hit shutout, 15-9 career vs. Twins; Konerko added 38th homer
Sept. 26		@ Detroit	L	4-3	Cliff Politte	94-62	Garland (6 2/3 IP, 8 H) 1-5 in last 9 starts; Konerko, Crede homer before Granderson's GW HR off Politte
Sept. 27	D	@ Detroit	L	3-2	Brandon McCarthy	94-63	Sox left 12 men on base and tying run at 2nd in 9th; maintained 2-game lead over Indians with 5 left
Sept. 28		@ Detroit	W	8-2	Jose Contreras	95-63	Contreras (8 IP, 7 H, 0 BB) struck out season-high 9; Uribe, Rowand padded lead with late-inning HRs
Sept. 29		@ Detroit	W	4-2	Freddy Garcia	96-63	Everett's 2-run triple in 1st put Sox ahead early; Konerko slammed 40th homer as Sox clinch Central
Sept. 30		@ Cleveland	W	3-2 (13)	Cliff Politte	97-63	Gload's 2-run double in 13th helped Sox clinch home-field advantage throughout playoffs
Oct. 1	C	@ Cleveland	W	4-3	Jon Garland	98-63	Sox scored 4 in 7th capped by Iguchi's 3-run homer, improved to 9-0 in 1-run games with Indians
Oct. 2		@ Cleveland	W	3-1	Brandon McCarthy	99-63	Dye hit team's 200th homer of season; Sox tie 1983 team for 2nd most wins in team history

AMERICAN LEAGUE DIVISION SERIES

	OPPONENT		SCORE		PITCHER OF RECORD	REC.	QUICK HIT
Oct. 4		Boston	W	14-2	Jose Contreras	100-63	Five Sox homers, tying a postseason record, led by Pierzynski's 2 shots and Podsednik's 1st of year
Oct. 5	B	Boston	W	5-4	Mark Buehrle	101-63	Sox homer once, but Iguchi's 3-run HR capped 5-run 5th inning while Buehrle (7 IP, 8 H, 4 ER) settled in
Oct. 7		at Boston	W	5-3	Freddy Garcia	102-63	Konerko HR broke tie in 6th; Hernandez in relief shut down Red Sox with 3-inning appearance

AMERICAN LEAGUE CHAMPIONSHIP SERIES

	OPPONENT		SCORE		PITCHER OF RECORD	REC.	QUICK HIT
Oct. 11		L.A. Angels	L	3-2	Jose Contreras	102-64	Contreras (8 1/3 IP, 3 R) solid, but Crede's HR, Pierzynski single only White Sox runs off Byrd
Oct. 12		L.A. Angels	W	2-1	Mark Buehrle	103-64	Disputed 3rd out of Pierzynski in 9th opened door for Crede GW double; Buehrle has 5-hit CG
Oct. 14	A	@ L.A. Angels	W	5-2	Jon Garland	104-64	Garland went distance allowing 4 hits while Konerko 2-run HR in 1st jump-started offense
Oct. 15		@ L.A. Angels	W	8-2	Freddy Garcia	105-64	Garcia pitched 3rd straight complete game; Konerko hit 3-run HR in 1st as offense came alive
Oct. 16		@ L.A. Angels	W	6-3	Jose Contreras	106-64	Contreras fired another complete game as Sox rallied from 3-2 down in 7th

WORLD SERIES

	OPPONENT		SCORE		PITCHER OF RECORD	REC.	QUICK HIT
Oct. 22		Houston	W	5-3	Jose Contreras	107-64	Crede big in field and at the plate, his solo HR giving Sox a 4-3 lead in the 4th
Oct. 23		Houston	W	7-6	Mark Buehrle	108-64	Blew 6-4 lead in top of 9th, but Podsednik's solo HR with 1 out in 9th won it
Oct. 25		@ Houston	W	7-5 (14)	Jon Garland	109-64	In longest World Series game in history, Blum's 2-out solo HR in 14th broke 5-5 tie
Oct. 26		@ Houston	W	1-0	Freddy Garcia	110-64	Garcia spun 7 strong innings; Dye's 2-out single in 8th drove in game's only run

Chicago Tribune Believe It! The Story of Chicago's World Champions

Publisher: David Hiller
Editor: Ann Marie Lipinski
Managing editor: James O'Shea
Deputy managing editor, news: George de Lama

Sports editors: Dan McGrath, Bill Adee
Photo editors: John Konstantaras, Todd Panagopoulos
Art directors: Catherine Nichols, Chuck Burke
Copy editors: Lucy Hoy, Tom Carkeek, Rich Strom, Mike Kellams, Mike Kates, Mike Sansone, Chris Kuc, Bob Vanderberg, Lee Gordon
Imaging: Don Bierman, Kathy Celer, Christine Bruno
Statistics: Keith Claxton, Steve Layton
Project managers: Bill Parker, Tony Majeri, Susan Zukrow
Out Loud interviews: Steve Rosenbloom

Photographers:
Charles Cherney: 4-5, 8, 16-17, 18, 22, 38 (top), 40-41, 43, 45, 46-47, 49, 52-53, 53 (bottom), 56-57 (all), 59, 70-71, 74-75, 80-81, 85 (bottom), 88-89, 92-93, 104-105, 110 (center, top center, bottom center), 118-119
Candice Cusic: 112
Nuccio DiNuzzo: Cover, 15, 20-21, 24, 37, 60-61, 66 (bottom), 72-73, 73 (bottom), 78-79, 85 (top), 99, 108-109, 110-111, back cover
Terrence Antonio James: 8-9, 96 (bottom), 105 (top)
John Lee: 28-29, 32
José Osorio: 38 (bottom), 53 (top), 55, 66-67, 76, 82-83, 90, 90-91, 94-95, 95, 100-101, 103, 105 (bottom), 114 (all)
Wes Pope: 115 (bottom)
John Smierciak: 36

Scott Strazzante: 2-3, 13, 23, 26-27, 30-31, 33, 34-35, 50-51, 54, 65, 66 (top), 68, 68-69, 84-85, 86 (all), 87, 101 (bottom), 106-107, 108, 109, 110 (top left, top right, middle left, middle right, bottom left, bottom right), 112-113, 116-117
Tribune Archives: 121 (all)
Abel Uribe: 11
Phil Velasquez: 1, 19, 39, 42, 44, 48, 62-63, 73 (top)
Jason Wambsgans: 6-7, 10, 12, 14, 96-97, 102-103, 115 (top)

The accounts in this book are based on the reporting of Dan McGrath, Mark Gonzales, Phil Rogers, David Haugh, Fred Mitchell, Paul Sullivan, Melissa Isaacson and Dave van Dyck